JACK MONROE
VEGAN(ish)

JACK MONROE
VEGAN(ish)

100 simple budget recipes that don't cost the earth

bluebird
books for life

Contents

Introduction

I first adopted a more plant-based diet in January 2016, and like most of my adventures, I didn't do it by halves. I went vegan for Veganuary, and loved the new life and colour that my cookery took on. I encouraged my household to follow suit, and they attempted it with enthusiasm and an open mind.

But as a food writer working primarily with families on very low incomes and food bank users, my work and lifestyle can never be described as 'completely' vegan. I no longer use the label to describe myself, because it doesn't quite fit, like a shirt two sizes too small. Instead, I create mostly vegan recipes that are simple, affordable, and accessible – hoping to encourage more people to consume fewer animal products through temptation and seduction, rather than guilt and self-loathing.

My theory is, if all of us adopted a few more plant-based meals into our diets on a weekly basis, not only would our food bills go down, but so would our environmental impact, and the demand for animal products would naturally decrease. Many of my readers now describe themselves as 'mostly vegan', due in part to a surfeit of readily available, non-threatening, easy meal ideas.

So you won't find any guilt trips within these pages – just a collection of (mostly) very simple, affordable, encouraging recipes, that no matter if you're looking to ditch meat altogether, cook for a vegan relative or friend, or are intolerant to dairy products, I hope there will be something here for you to experiment with and adore, and surprise and delight yourself.

There is a false equivalency, especially on social media, with veganism, plant-based diets, and 'clean eating'. These recipes are naturally packed with fruit, veg and nutrients by virtue of being made from plants, but they aren't claiming to be anything other than delicious. There are plenty of riffs on everyday classic recipes, such as the Big Jack and the Breakfast MuckMuffin, Bakewell Tarts and Birthday Cake, to put to rest any ideas about virtue or purity

here. I like food in all its guises – from bold crunchy salads to dripping sloppy buns, and everything in between.

There may be a few unfamiliar ingredients, but don't let that put you off – there's a handy A-Z guide over the next few pages that will talk you through where to find them and what they can be used for. The herbs and spices used in this book are slightly more extensive than my previous tomes, but not excessively so. You may be surprised to find me using agar, chestnuts and saffron in a 'budget' cookbook – and I admit I hesitated to include the latter, so have made it firmly optional rather than essential. I found when I started to reduce the amount of meat and dairy products in my shopping basket, which are comparatively expensive, there was a little financial flexibility that allowed for a few 'luxury' ingredients.

And as with all of my recipes, if you want to un-veganize them, feel free, I'm not going to sulk about it. This book is here as a guide to show you how to make incredible vegan food with very little effort – but if you want to switch one kind of milk out for another, or cheese, or whatever, use them as a base to play with. I write guidelines, not prescriptions.

When you make these recipes, do post them on social media and tag me – I absolutely love to see my creations brought to life by your fair hands, it brings me so much puppyish glee every single time! I'm on instagram @jack_monroe and Twitter @bootstrapcook – get in touch!

Jack
x

**You don't have to be vegan every day.
But every single day you are,
you save, on average:**

———————

ONE ANIMAL

40 POUNDS OF GRAIN

1100 GALLONS OF WATER

30 SQUARE FEET OF FOREST

———————

Together, our 'one days' can add up
to a massive change

For us, for animal welfare,
and for our planet

(Statistics from thevegancalculator.com and Cowspiracy.com/facts)

Equipment

I try to keep the equipment chapters of my cookbooks as short and as simple as possible, with everyday, affordable recommendations, and this one is no exception. You don't need lots of fancy shiny gear in order to cook from scratch; I prefer to prioritize worktop space and a sense of calm over a cluttered environment, although I do admit to having a few more pans and spoons than those listed here. I have specific recommendations for each item here, so if you go to jackmonroe.com and type 'Equipment' into the search bar, it will bring up links to the things I use and love – bear in mind I test and develop recipes for a living so will use each around ten times more than the average household, so if it has survived my kitchen, it's well worth it!

Pans
1 large deep nonstick saucepan
1 small deep nonstick saucepan
1 large frying or sauté pan, preferably with a lid

In the oven
A large roasting tin or two
A small roasting tin
A square cake tin, for cakes and brownies
A loaf tin

In the drawer
Two wooden spoons
A masher
General cutlery
Small sharp knife
Vegetable peeler
A whisk
Large heavy chefs knife
Hand-held grater
Box grater

Vegan(ish)

Small measuring jug
Tongs for tossing and turning
Turner for veggie burgers etc
Rubber spatula

On the worktop
Large mixing bowl or two

Small bullet blender – by far the best investment I have ever
made in my kitchen, mine was £25 from a housewares store and
is an exact imitation of its fancy counterpart – it has lasted three
cookbooks and half a dozen uses a day. The £150 one lasted three
months before it blew up – literally – in a haze of smoke. Make
of that what you will! Be sure to clean it regularly and thoroughly,
and don't run it for too long at a time, and it will last ages.

Digital scales – and a few spare batteries too, as they always seem
to run out at the least convenient times.

And the rest
Airtight containers for storing leftovers
A few clean glass jars with lids for making salad dressings
and storing odds and sods
Measuring cups and spoons if you like to be precise
A notebook and pen for jotting down your own twists,
tweaks and ideas

A Whole New World
An A to Z of Veganism, or Vegan(ish), or Just Eating More Plants

Agar agar This is a jelly-forming substance, harvested from red algae. I use it in making jelly, the same way that gelatine would traditionally be used in old-style cookery. If you think that seaweed or algae sounds grim, well, I'd take it over boiled up hooves any day! It's used in the 'Pork Belly' recipe on pages 172–4 to form the gelatinous, fat-marbling layer. It's fairly heat resistant at high temperatures, and you can use it in sweet or savoury dishes. The little flakes go a long way and last well if stored in a clean, airtight container, so although they may seem pricey for an initial ingredient, it's worth the investment. For a cheaper option, try Vege-gel from the baking aisle of most major supermarkets.

Aquafaba This is the thick, viscous liquid that canned pulses have been stored in, and has enjoyed a surge in popularity over recent years as a miracle vegan product. It can be used to make mayonnaise, as an egg replacer in baking, and for light and crisp meringues (see page 201). Chickpea aquafaba is the most commonly used, but I prefer cannellini – I find the taste lighter and less intrusive in sweet baking. I have experimented with many beans, legumes and pulses and would only recommend cannellini and chickpea for cooking – kidney beans, black beans and the like are out of the question! You get about 125ml of aquafaba from one tin of beans.

Butter (equivalents) For spreading on bread or toast, I like Pure dairy free spread, Vitalite, Flora freedom range and avocado spread by Aldi, as a treat. For frying, I use sunflower oil or rapeseed oil, as they are both virtually tasteless. For making pastry, I use vegetable oil, with the exception of puff pastry, where I use vegan margarine that has been popped in the freezer for 20 minutes to chill and firm it.

B12 supplement Vegan diets can lack in vitamin B12 as plant-based sources of B12 are difficult to absorb, so I take a supplement. You need enough vitamin B12 for your red blood cells to form properly and transport oxygen around the body. If you don't get enough B12, it can lead to a kind of anaemia (pernicious anaemia) – so if follow a vegan diet full-time, please do take a B12 supplement and consider checking your B12 levels with a doctor.

Cheese I have tried many, many vegan 'cheeses' and let me save you the disappointment, some of them are truly nasty. Sorry, but I'd rather you found out from these pages than from your tastebuds and wasted wallet. The ones I use with regularity that never disappoint are as follows. For a good all-rounder that melts well, Follow Your Heart Cheddar Shreds. The smoked version is phenomenally good. Violife mozzarella-flavour slices are good on pizza, but I find I need to use quite a few to get a good gooey texture going. Asda garlic and herb 'cheese' is brilliant crumbled into salads, dips or on crackers. For a Parmesan equivalent, Violife hard strong cheese is the one to go for grated over pasta – it makes a convincing enough cacio e pepe, and that's good enough for me. There is a recipe on page 120 for Smoky Vegan 'Cheese' Sauce for pasta and dips, and one on pages 98–9 for Vegan Ricotta – so get stuck in!

Applewood smoked cheese ✔

Chicken-style stock You may see reference to chicken-style stock throughout this book – this is not a typo! Many good vegan 'chicken' stocks exist, and my favourite of all of them is Osem, which comes in a large tub of bouillon-style powder. It makes a satisfyingly chicken-y base for soups, pasta dishes, and any savoury meals that need a base note of indeterminable flavour – you can find it in most supermarkets, or online, either with the stocks or in the Kosher or Halal food section.

Children My son tried veganism with the enthusiasm of adorable progeny trying desperately to please his mother, but after a few weeks quietly mumbled that he wanted some proper sausages again. I wrestled with it, but after laying out the facts, he decided to spend his own pocket money on sausages and fish fingers, and I appreciated his grown-up response and cooked his dinner for him. Nowadays, he eats meat and fish two or three times a week, but will eat Linda McCartney veggie sausages with gusto, and requests my vegan sausage rolls on a regular basis. Children have their own agency, and I encourage him to make his own decisions.

Vitamin D supplement Vitamin D has many functions in the body but most of us know it's required for healthy bones, teeth and muscles – all of which are kind of essential! Our bodies create vitamin D through UV radiation in sunlight on our skin, from about March to September but in the winter months, when the days are shorter, it's vital to eat a diet rich in vitamin D and supplement to compensate for the lack of sunlight. Vitamin D has two major forms, D3 and D2. Vitamin D3 is found in small amounts in animal sources, such as oily fish, beef liver, cheese and egg yolks. Vitamin D2 is the vegan type and is mostly found in mushrooms exposed to UV light – which is a bit limited! For this reason, I take a Vitamin D2 supplement to be on the safe side, and eat lots of mushrooms! Most plant-based 'milks', spreads and cereals are fortified with vitamin D but check when buying them.

Egg substitutes For meringues, baking and pastry glaze, see 'aquafaba' above. You can also get vegan egg equivalents from supermarkets and health food stores, such as Follow Your Heart Vegan Egg, but these can be pricey! Apple sauce and banana work well in pancakes, cakes, muffins and brownies. Mashed potato helps bind vegan burgers or 'meatloaf'. Medium firm tofu can be used in place of scrambled egg for breakfast – and in my Classic 'Egg' Sandwich on page 67.

Fake meat Each to their own, but I don't generally buy the whole 'fake meat' myself, unless for a bacon sandwich or the occasional cocktail sausage, but mostly because I would happily live off cocktail sausages and bacon sandwiches if given the choice, so I leave it out in order to continually challenge myself as a food writer. That said, it's a handy reference point for new vegans, or even those who want to try to cut down on their meat intake.

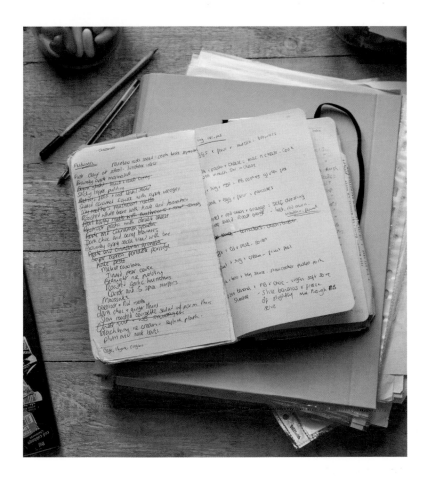

Some people might ask 'why do vegans want to eat something that tastes like meat' and instead I flip the question back at them: 'with alternatives available, why would you choose the barbaric option?'

Jackfruit Young, unripe jackfruit is increasingly used in plant-based cookery due to its meaty texture and neutral taste; with the right marinade it can imitate pulled pork, slow cooked beef, or shredded chicken. You can find it in tins in most large supermarkets – Summer Pride is my favourite brand. Some tinned jackfruit is tougher than others, and will need a good salty boil to tenderize it before using.

Kale A 'super food' (not to be confused with 'superfood', a term I wrinkle my nose at), kale is packed with vitamins, particularly vitamins A, C and K whch help to support a healthy immune system. It's relatively inexpensive to buy, especially frozen and I tend to sling it into soups, stews, pasta, curries or with garlic and lemon as a side dish.

Lentils The most common lentils are red, green and brown, used in a variety of dishes. As a rule, I use brown as a mince substitute, sometimes with a dash of gravy powder in a bolognese or lasagne. Red lentils swell and soften, so they are brilliant in soups and daals. Green lentils retain a good solid texture, making them ideal for a side dish, especially one with strong flavours, like herbs and tomato or red wine, or cooked in stock with garlic and lemon.

Milk Everyone has their favourite milk substitutes, and here are mine. In coffee and on cereal, I like vanilla soya milk by Alpro. For a mocha or hot chocolate, or in cakes, hazelnut milk is tremendous. For tea, hemp milk works well, as does soya, but I find that I need a lot more than 'ordinary' milk due to the high water content. Oat milk is good in cereals and smoothies, and cashew milk is thick and sweet and makes an excellent cheese sauce.

Miso A paste made from fermented soya beans, miso is often used in Japanese cooking. It can be thinned into a soup, or used as a marinade, and is my secret ingredient for adding depth and 'meaty' flavour to vegan dishes – from soups to stews to burgers and more. I prefer brown miso, as a little tiny bit goes a long way, but for those of you not used to the taste, start with white miso, which is sweeter and lighter, and work your way from there. You can buy it from most supermarkets, and it lasts a long time and packs quite a hefty amount of flavour into a small dollop!

Mushrooms These are low in calories and a source of the B vitamins B2, B3, B5 and even Vitamin D (if they've been exposed to sunlight – check the label). Mushrooms absolutely fascinate me, BBC Four aired a documentary called *The Magic of Mushrooms* in 2014, and I must have watched it, rapt with wonder, about a dozen times. Every kind of edible mushroom has a place on my dinner plate. Shiitake are dense and meaty, so good for making burgers, or as a meat replacement in a bourguignon, stroganoff or other hefty stew. Oyster mushrooms are delicate and beautiful, ideal for stir-frying or when you want to impress. Chestnut mushrooms are deep and nutty, button mushrooms firm and with a light flavour, and portobello mushrooms are the big ones ideal for roasting, stuffing or just slinging between two halves of a burger bun with a dollop of ketchup and mustard and a shrug. Mushrooms are so versatile, I try to include them in my diet three times a week, for breakfast, on toast, in a deep-filled toastie, in stews, casseroles, curries and more. I could write more but you get the idea. My close friend Georgi is violently allergic to mushrooms – and it is a testament to the strength of our friendship that I will exorcise all trace of them from my kitchen to cook for her now and again.

Nuts Tiny little powerhouses of proteins, fibre and essential fats, nuts have a vital combination of nutrients. Adding flavour, texture and thickness to a variety of dishes, almonds are also a good source of vitamin E, cashew nuts are high in protein, iron and zinc. Chestnuts are the lowest of all the nut family in fat and calories, and high in fibre, and B vitamins. Hazelnuts are a good source of folate and vitamin B6. Just a small handful serving of walnuts per day can contribute to the elasticity of blood vessels – helping to reduce blood pressure. Pistachios are high in fibre and potassium, and vitamin B6. You can make your own nut butters, add them to sweet and savoury dishes or keep them on hand as a snack.

Oats A nutrient-dense food, the humble oat provides a good source of carbohydrates and fibre, protein and contains unsaturated fatty acids. Oats are also a source of manganese, magnesium, copper, iron, zinc and thiamin. Interestingly, due to their beta-glucan content (a special type of fibre) a serving of oats per day could help to lower your cholesterol.

Omega-3 fatty acids These are essential fats. They are usually associated with oily fish, such as salmon or mackerel, due to being a rich source of omega-3 fatty acids. However, a type of omega 3 can also be found in a variety of vegan sources. There are in general, three kinds of omega 3 fatty acids called alpha-linoleic acid (ALA), docosahexaenoic acid (DHA) and eicosapentaenoic acid

(EPA). Typically, our body only uses DHA and EPA but it can create both DHA and EPA from ALA. it is thought to be important for overall health to get a variety of each of the fatty acids. In terms of vegan sources, nuts and seeds are rich in ALA and seaweed can provide a little EPA. Nori and seaweed and other sea vegetables are now found in most supermarkets – take a peek in the world foods aisle near the Japanese cookery ingredients to find it. ALA sources of omega 3 fatty acids include most seeds and their oils, such as: hemp seed, chia seed, flaxseed, rapeseed and sunflower seed. Walnuts, edamame (soya) beans and kidney beans also contain some ALA, some of which can be found at supermarkets and some you may need to track down in a health-food store if you fancy them. I get my omega 3 by eating kidney beans, frozen edamame, walnuts and crispy crunchy seaweed snacks, so trekking around for the hard to find ingredients is by no means essential.

Protein One of the most common questions asked of people following a vegan diet, is 'where do you get your protein from?' I usually roll my eyes and say 'the same place as orangutans get theirs from – plants' and go about my day. But for those looking for a more comprehensive answer, there are many, many plant-based sources of protein available to you. Seitan (a meat alternative made from wheat protein), tofu and tempeh can all be used to replace meat in most recipes. Edamame beans are delicious, and can be bought cheaply from the frozen section of the supermarket. Beans and pulses, such as chickpeas, kidney beans, black beans, lentils, nuts and all other legumes contain around 15–18g of protein per cup. Soya milk, oats and nuts are also a sources of protein. There are also a wide range of vegan protein powders based on pea, brown rice or other plant-based proteins, but the truth is if you include some of the sources I mentioned 2–3 times a day and incorporate a wide variety of vegetables in your diet, including broccoli, spinach, potatoes, sweet potatoes, sprouts, asparagus and artichokes (if you feel fancy) – you're not likely to be protein-deficient any time soon and probably don't need to supplement.

Vegan(ish)

Restaurants Most friends of mine who are chefs, which is quite a lot of them, relish the challenge of catering for vegan diners – BUT it is considered courteous to let them know in advance if there is a large party of guests with any specific dietary requirements. I do my research beforehand – most menus are online nowadays – to save the agony of asking a thousand questions once I'm seated and hungry. When I have the menu in my hands, I use it as a shopping list of ingredients, and cobble together starters and sides, ask for dishes without the meat/fish/cheese if possible, or simply point at some things I like and ask very nicely if the chef could make something vegan with those flavours. A little politeness and a big grin goes a long way, and always tip generously for the effort. Who knows, whatever comes out of the kitchen could end up on the menu!

Umami According to Dara Ó Briain's brilliant book *Secret Science*, 'Umami is the Japanese word for deliciousness and, alongside sweet, salty, sour and bitter, is one of the five tastes that make up all of our foods'. When I was writing this book, my then-nine year-old son, standing behind me, parroted this verbatim. I almost fell off my chair in shock that firstly, he knew what 'umami' meant, and secondly, I couldn't take the credit for it! Umami is a deeply savoury flavour, and in vegan cookery, can be obtained from soy sauce-based dishes, slow-cooked broths, meaty mushroom notes, yeast extract and dark miso paste.

Xanthan gum Usually found in the 'free from' aisle at the supermarket, xanthan gum is a thickening agent and stabilizer, useful for binding technically difficult recipes, such as vegan meringues, when sometimes no matter how much you whisk, they just won't pull together. A little goes a very long way.

One

Bread and Breakfast

'Cheese' and Marmite Giant Scone

Makes 1 giant scone, serves 6–8

3 tbsp cooking oil, plus extra for greasing

225g self-raising flour

A pinch each of salt and black pepper

2 tbsp Marmite or other inferior yeast extract

150ml your favourite vegan 'milk' (see intro)

50g vegan mature 'cheese'

Marmite is an excellent source of vital vitamins and minerals in a vegan diet, or at least, that's my excuse for shovelling the black stuff into my face by the teaspoon when prowling my kitchen looking for a snack. I brought this scone along on the day we photographed the cover for this book, and the team was much larger than I realised. We cut it into slivers, but they were slivers that everyone raved about, and the smell of Marmitey baked goodness lingered hungrily in the air of the studio for the rest of the day. I've left the milk and cheese elements of this recipe deliberately ambiguous so as not to be too prescriptive; every vegan I've met has their own favourite types, but I'll offer some guidance as to my own personal tastes. For milk, soya works fine – both the refrigerated and the UHT varieties. Soya light has variable results. Almond and coconut 'milks' tend to be a little on the sweet side for this, but if that's what you fancy, go for it. Violife mature Cheddar-flavour block would be my choice here, and it's available in most supermarkets. Bute Island mature Cheddar-style grated Sheese is a good shout, too.

1 First grab a large mixing bowl, and turn your oven on to 200°C (fan 180°C/400°F/gas 6). Lightly grease a 20cm round cake tin or decent-sized loaf tin (about 450g), and set to one side.

2 Measure the flour into the bowl and add the salt and pepper. Pour in the oil, and add the Marmite, 'milk' and 'cheese'. Mix well to form a tacky dough; I use a rubber spatula for this, as a wooden spoon tends to get clogged up, but either will do.

3 When all the ingredients are well combined, tip and scrape them into the cake or loaf tin, and pop in the oven on the centre shelf for 25 minutes to cook, until risen and golden.

4 Allow to cool for 15 minutes in the tin before turning out to serve. Serve immediately, or cool completely and store in an airtight container for up to 3 days. It can also be frozen for up to 3 months.

Vegan(ish)

Apricot and Sunflower Seed Granola

You can vary the fruit and seeds in this granola to suit what you have in your kitchen or your personal tastes, and those looking to reduce their sugar intake can halve the golden syrup quantity by boiling 100g syrup with 100ml water to loosen it. If you do this, it will need slightly longer in the oven, as it starts off wetter than the original recipe.

———————

1 First preheat the oven to 180°C (fan 160°C/350°F/gas 4) and lightly grease a baking tray. Measure the golden syrup into a large mixing bowl and add the cooking oil and cinnamon, and mix well to combine.

2 Tip in the oats, add the sunflower seeds and mix thoroughly to ensure all the oats are coated in the syrup mixture.

3 Finely chop the apricots and pumpkin seeds, and scatter them on top of the oats and sunflower seeds. Fold in carefully, making sure they are evenly distributed throughout the mixture.

4 Spoon the mixture onto the baking tray and bake in the centre of the oven for 14 minutes, removing halfway through to turn with a spatula to cook it evenly.

5 When the granola is golden and crisp at the edges, remove it from the oven and cool completely before transferring to a clean (preferably sterile, see tip below) storage jar. Use within 3 weeks.

Makes 10 servings

———————

4 tbsp cooking oil, plus extra for greasing

200g golden syrup

1 tsp ground cinnamon

300g porridge oats

70g sunflower seeds

200g dried apricots

30g pumpkin seeds

You can sterilize jars with Milton fluid, used for cleaning baby bottles and useful to keep in any frugal kitchen for sterilizing jars for leftovers, pickles and preserves. Or you can wash them with hot soapy water and bake in the oven for 10 minutes at 120°C (fan 100°C/250°F/gas ½), leaving in the warm oven until required

Vegan Brioche

Makes 1 large loaf

———————

1 tbsp gram flour

3 tbsp aquafaba
(see page 12)

2 tbsp light cooking oil, plus
extra for greasing

250g plain flour, plus
extra for dusting

100g vegan spread

10g dried active yeast

A generous pinch of salt

2 tbsp caster sugar

200ml warm water

A little vegan 'milk' or oil,
to glaze (optional)

Making a vegan brioche was one of my absolute goals for this book; a combination of sheer greed and impetuous determination to nail that soft, buttery, light yet sumptuous loaf. It took a few attempts, eventually leading to what I christened the '123 Egg' in my head – and now, here, out loud. I occasionally take quite an analytical approach to cookery, and when I am flummoxed by a new idea, I deconstruct it, stripping it down to its core function and component parts. (It's this method of breaking down ingredients one at a time that led me to replace red wine with black tea in casserole one evening, and with success.) So for this, I stood in my kitchen, leaning on the worktop, jotting down the key roles that an egg typically plays in a recipe. Protein, flavour and a binding agent. A slight sweetness from the yolk. Unctuous, and slightly gelatinous. I scoured my shelves and started to experiment. One tablespoon of gram flour, two of light cooking oil, and three of aquafaba seemed to do the trick, and lends a glorious golden colour, too.

———————

1 First make your vegan 'egg' replacer. Measure the gram flour, aquafaba and cooking oil into a small bowl and beat well to combine. Set to one side.

2 Weigh the flour into a large mixing bowl. Add the vegan spread a little at a time to make it easier to incorporate. Rub the spread and the flour between your fingers to form a fine breadcrumb consistency, until all the spread is incorporated roughly evenly. Measure in the yeast, and add the salt and sugar. Stir briefly to distribute evenly.

3 Stir together the vegan spread mix and warm water to make a liquid – I do this in a small bullet blender for ease – then stir in the vegan egg mixture until well combined.

4 Flour your worktop and knead the dough well for a few minutes until it starts to feel springy in your hands. Cut the dough in half to make two pieces, then cut each into four to make eight pieces of dough. Roll each into a soft ball.

5 Lightly grease a small round cake tin, I used a 20cm one. Pop one dough ball in the middle and arrange the other seven around the outside. Cover with a clean, large mixing bowl and leave to stand in a warm place for 4 hours or until doubled in size.

6 When doubled in size, glaze the top with a little 'milk' or oil, if you like. Heat the oven to 160°C (fan 140°/325°F/gas 3). Place the cake tin on the middle shelf and bake for 25 minutes or until risen and golden.

7 Remove from the oven and cool in the tin for 15 minutes, before removing to a wire rack to cool completely. This keeps for 2–3 days in an airtight storage container or freezer bag. It freezes well too – if you slice it before freezing, it can be toasted from frozen like regular bread.

Crumpets

I very rarely advocate the use of specialist equipment in my recipes, but egg-poaching rings are very handy for making crumpets. I picked mine up for £1 from a well-known hardware and home store, and they have lasted a good few years so far, so I consider them a worthy investment. You could make a giant crumpet in a frying pan, I suppose, but it would be ambitious. They take a little practice and patience, both of which I sorely lack at the best of times, but they're worth it!

1 Grab a large mixing bowl and weigh your flour into it. Add the yeast and bicarbonate of soda, and a little salt and pepper, and mix well to evenly distribute the ingredients.

2 Mix together the water and 'milk'. Make a well in the centre of the flour base, and add the wet ingredients. Stir well to form a loose batter. Cover and leave to rise in a warm place for an hour.

3 Gently heat a non-stick frying pan and place the egg-poaching rings into it. Add a dollop of oil to each one, and turn the heat down to the lowest possible setting. Dollop 3 tablespoons of the mixture into each poaching ring and leave to cook for 12 minutes. It is agonisingly slow, but so beautiful and satisfying to watch, I consider it particularly therapeutic to just gaze at them and watch the bubbles rise and burst, rise, and gently burst. You'll be tempted to turn them over; don't yet, as you will lose the beautiful holes. When the last of the batter has solidified on the top, flip them over and crank up the heat for the last minute. Set to one side and repeat as required.

4 I serve mine with lashings of vegan spread and Marmite, but you are free to smother them in whatever you wish, within reason. These keep for 2–3 days in an airtight storage container or freezer bag. They freeze well too, but for best results defrost completely before cooking, and reheat in the oven, not the toaster.

Makes 10

———————

300g plain flour

2 tbsp dried active yeast

1 tsp bicarbonate of soda

A generous pinch of salt and black pepper

200ml warm water

300ml vegan 'milk' – I used soya

Cooking oil, for frying

To serve

Vegan spread

Marmite or jam

Peanut Butter and Banana Breakfast Bars

Makes 8 generous bars

————————

Cooking oil, for greasing

3 large ripe bananas

250g peanut butter, crunchy or smooth

5 tbsp golden syrup, plus extra for drizzling (optional)

1 tsp ground cinnamon (optional)

½ tsp grated nutmeg (optional)

200g porridge oats

These simple breakfast bars are a hit with my young son, who helps me to make and eat them with equal enthusiasm! Easy to grab on the go in the mornings on the school run, or as an afternoon snack, I leave them on the kitchen counter and they disappear within a day or two. We have made several varieties – replacing the syrup with strawberry or blackcurrant jam for an American-inspired PBJ twist, varying the spices, adding mixed fruits; you can adjust this recipe to your taste and storecupboard.

————————

1 First heat your oven to 190°C (fan 170°C/375°F/gas 5), and lightly grease a deep 20cm square cake tin, or one of similar proportions.

2 Vigorously mash your bananas, peanut butter and syrup together in either a mixing bowl or small bullet blender for a smoother result. Add the spices, if using, and stir through. Add the oats and fold into the mixture, making sure they are all coated in the banana-peanut butter mixture.

3 Spoon the mixture into the greased cake tin and flatten with a spatula or wooden spoon, pressing it into all four corners and evening out the top. Drizzle with extra syrup, if you like.

4 Bake in the centre of the oven for 45 minutes, until golden and firming at the edges.

5 Remove from the oven and cool in the tin for 30 minutes, before dividing into bars with a sharp heavy knife. Remove carefully with a spatula or palette knife and transfer to a wire rack to cool. Store in an airtight container for up to 4 days, or freeze for 3 months.

Vegan(ish)

Banana and Berry Baked Oats

Baked oats are a healthy breakfast that feels like a dessert — what's not to love? You can mix them up and leave them in the fridge overnight like a Bircher pot, then pop them into the oven in the morning when you wake. By the time you've finished your morning shower and got dressed, the smell of starchy sweetness will coax even the most stubborn of breakfast refuseniks into the kitchen. The berries can be replaced with any of your choice, or more bananas, or cinnamon and other spices -— or even a couple of dollops of red or purple jam. Works well with gluten-free oats, too.

<hr>

1 First make your banana milk; peel the bananas and break them into chunks into the large cup of a small bullet blender, then add the 'milk' and 'yoghurt'. Blitz to a smooth, thick liquid.

2 Pour the liquid into a mixing bowl, making sure to scrape every last drop out of the blender cup. Add the oats and stir thoroughly to coat. Taste the mixture — if it is sweet enough for your liking, great! If not, you can add a little sugar or your chosen sweetener to taste.

3 Pour the berries into a small deep oven dish or round cake tin (approx 18cm). Spoon the banana-oat mixture on top. Either chill in the fridge until required, or bake straight away. If baking straight away, pop on the centre shelf of the oven at 180°C (fan 160°C/350°F/gas 4) for 40 minutes. If cooking from chilled, allow 45 minutes. You may wish to put a baking tray on the bottom of the oven or the shelf beneath, as this can get a little excitable and bubble over the sides! Serve warm.

Serves 2

<hr>

2 large very ripe bananas, or 3 small–medium ones

100ml vegan 'milk' — soya, almond and oat all work well

150g plain vegan 'yoghurt'

50g instant oats

Sugar or sweetener, to taste (optional)

150g frozen mixed berries

I love these served warm, with a splash of vegan 'milk' for breakfast, but you could also have them with vegan custard or ice cream for dessert

Pear and Ginger Pancakes

Makes 12

---

1 x 400g tin of pears, approx

225g self-raising flour

1½ tsp bicarbonate of soda

1 tbsp sugar

1 tsp ground ginger

½ tsp ground cinnamon

1 tbsp cooking oil,
plus extra for frying

120ml your favourite
vegan 'milk'

To serve (optional)

Lemon juice

Sugar

Maple syrup

On Sundays in my small household, we have pancakes. Usually eaten in bed, en famille, with a large ginger cat poking his nose in, and every Sunday they are different to the last. These came about from a pondering whether pear sauce would work in the same way as applesauce as an egg replacement, and setting about making some from a tin of pears. Behold, it worked, and these beautiful, and very simple, pancakes were born. For the milk in this recipe I used cashew, as it's what I had at the time, but any vegan 'milk' (or indeed non-vegan, if that's your jam) will suffice. A handful of mixed peel, if you have it, makes these extra special.

---

1 First blend your tinned pears to make a smooth sauce. Empty the entire tin, including the juice, into a small bullet blender and pulse until smooth. Pour this into a small saucepan and simmer for around 15 minutes, until the contents have reduced by a third and are thick and smell delicious. Stir it every now and then to stop it catching at the bottom of the pan and burning.

2 Turn your oven on to 120°C (fan 100°C/250°F/gas ½) and pop a baking tray on the centre shelf. Measure the flour, bicarb, sugar, ginger and cinnamon into a mixing bowl and stir well to combine. Make a well – a small hole – in the centre of the dry ingredients. Pour in the pear sauce, oil and 'milk' and beat thoroughly to form a smooth batter.

3 Heat a little oil in a large non-stick frying pan. When the oil is sizzling, dollop a dessertspoon of the mixture into it, and another one, and another one, leaving space for them to expand. Cook for 3 minutes on one side and then carefully, but quickly, turn over with a spatula. Don't worry if they scrumple up a little, mine frequently do; they taste all the same to me! Cook for 2 minutes on that side and then transfer carefully to the oven to keep warm and continue to gently cook.

4 Repeat until all the pancake batter is used up. Serve with lemon and sugar – immediately!

Vegan(ish)

Spiced Banana Bread

Makes 1 medium loaf

———————

5 tbsp cooking oil, plus
extra for greasing

50g sugar

Seeds from
6 cardamom pods

1 tsp ground anise or
2 star anise

3 ripe bananas

225g self-raising flour

2 tsp baking powder

3 tsp ground cinnamon

100g sultanas

Peanut butter and apple
slices, to serve (optional)

This simple banana bread is a level up from one of the most popular recipes in my first book, *A Girl Called Jack*, with some extra flavours to really make it sing. The cardamom and anise aren't essential if you're on a budget, but they add a warming, delicious base note, ideal for any time of the day with a nice cup of tea and a moment to yourself.

———————

1 Preheat your oven to 180°C (fan 160°C/350°F/gas 4) and lightly grease a 450g loaf tin.

2 Tip the sugar, cardamom seeds and anise into the blender and pulse for 30 seconds, pause, then pulse again. If using whole star anise it will make an atrocious rattling noise – this is normal, if slightly alarming. It is important not to run your blender with dry ingredients for more than 30 seconds at a time as they can sulk to the point of catching fire if the motor overheats!

3 When the spices are ground into the sugar, sift the mixture gently to remove any large lumps of woody star anise. I pop these into a new jar with some fresh sugar and the cardamom pods, and leave it to infuse for future cookies, mulled wine and more.

4 Peel and slice the bananas and pop them into a mixing bowl. If they aren't the old, squishy sort, add a little of the oil to soften them and start them off. Add the rest of the oil and the gently spiced sugar to the bowl, and mix well. It doesn't look too great at this stage but don't worry, it's normal and gets better. Tip in the flour, baking powder, cinnamon and sultanas, and stir well.

5 Pour the mixture into the loaf tin and bake for 1 hour in the centre of the oven, until the loaf is risen and golden. If a knife or a skewer inserted into the middle comes out clean, it's done.

6 For best results, cool completely in the tin before turning out to slice. Store, cooled, in foil, film or similar. Will keep for 2 days from fresh, and freezes well. I use leftovers as the base for a trifle, or blitz into crumbs to serve with ice cream.

Vegan(ish)

Breakfast Burritos

Makes 4 generous burritos

———————

1 large onion

1 × 400g tin of jackfruit in water – I like Summer Pride

1 tbsp smoked paprika

1 tbsp cumin, seeds or ground

1 tbsp any cooking oil

4 fat cloves of garlic

1 × 400g tin of black beans

1 × 400g tin of chopped tomatoes

100g plain white rice

A few handfuls lettuce

120g vegan 'cheese' (see intro note)

4 large tortilla wraps

To serve

Shop-bought guacamole
Shop-bought salsa

This recipe is known affectionately in my household as 'breakfast burritos', such is my penchant for making so much of the mixture that we usually end up having it for breakfast the next day as well. The defining characteristics of a classic burrito – at least, those that I have eaten in my lifetime, and that is a great number – is a tortilla wrapped into a closed-ended cylinder, stuffed generously with refried beans, slow-cooked meat, rice, any variation on cheese, salsa in a range of heats, lettuce and guacamole. I confess, to keep things simple, I buy in my guacamole and salsa most of the time. When I want to be a culinary martyr, I'll knock up my own, but most supermarkets make halfway decent versions of them these days.

For vegan 'cheese', I recommend Follow Your Heart Cheddar Shreds, or FYH Pepperjack-style slices for a Tex-Mex kick. For tortilla wraps, check the back of the packaging carefully – most supermarket wraps are suitable for vegans, but they occasionally contain milk, so keep an eye out.

———————

1 First peel and finely slice your onion, and toss into a large mixing bowl. Drain the jackfruit and thoroughly squeeze out any excess juices. Separate the jackfruit with your fingers and add to the onion. Sprinkle over the paprika and cumin, add the oil, and finely grate in the garlic. Drain the black beans and add to the bowl. Mix all together, cover and chill for at least an hour so it all marinates.

2 When the jackfruit, onions and beans have marinated, tip into a large, non-stick pan over a medium heat. Cook for 20 minutes, then pour over the tomatoes and cook for 20 minutes more.

3 Pour the rice into a medium saucepan and add double the volume of water. Bring to the boil, then simmer for 18–20 minutes, or until the rice is soft and swollen. Drain if needed (in an ideal world, the rice would absorb all of the water, but it took me a long

Vegan(ish)

time to get that right, so don't beat yourself up if there's a little water left in your pan), then set to one side.

4 Finely slice your lettuce and grate your 'cheese', and get your guacamole and salsa in position.

5 To assemble your burrito, lay the tortilla in one hand. Spoon rice into the centre, then beans, then add lettuce, 'cheese', guac and salsa. Fold up the bottom a quarter of the way up, then roll tightly into a cylinder, sealing with a dab of guac. Eat immediately, or chill for later, and enjoy.

Bread and Breakfast

Rainbow Fritters

Makes around 12,
depending on how large or
small you make them!

1 onion

1 courgette

2 carrots

1 beetroot

2 tbsp flour

1 tbsp aquafaba
(see page 12)

Salt and black pepper

Curry powder or ground
cumin, to taste (optional)

Cooking oil, for frying

I try to encourage my small family to eat the rainbow as early on in the day as possible, which saves us cramming half the plate with frozen mixed vegetables defrosted in a Pyrex jug in the microwave in the evening, for fear that we all get scurvy overnight. I am, in some respects, an anxious mother, but left to their own devices my brood would live on licorice toffee and chicken nuggets, so I have to take them in hand somehow. Breakfasts, especially on the weekends, are a colourful affair, and that's where the inspiration for this recipe came from. Eagle-eyed readers will recall courgette fritters in my first cookbook, *A Girl Called Jack*; these are a simplified vegan version. You can use any root vegetable for this recipe; some may take a little longer to cook than others.

1 First turn your oven on to 180°C/350°F/gas 4 and place a cookie sheet or baking tray on the middle shelf. This will be a storage rack for your fritters in a little while.

2 Grab a large mixing bowl and grate in the onion, followed by the courgette, and carrots. Grate the beetroot into a separate bowl for now, as it has a habit of turning everything else pink!

3 Spoon in the flour and a splash of aquafaba to make a batter to bind the veg together. Don't worry if it is a little loose at the moment, the beetroot needs to join in! Season the batter with salt and pepper, and add a spice if you like. Cumin works well, so does standard curry powder, but these are fine without either.

4 Dollop the beetroot in and fold it into the batter – that's stir it slowly and carefully without mixing it too much. Stand the mixture to one side for a moment.

5 Heat a little oil in a frying pan. Add a dollop of the mixture, around 2 tablespoons, and flatten gently with a fork. Cook on a medium–high heat for 3 minutes on each side, then carefully transfer each fritter to the oven. Repeat until all of the batter is used up. Cook the fritters in the oven for around 15 minutes, and serve hot.

Vegan(ish)

Breakfast MuckMuffin

I started with a standard McMuffin as my point of reference for this recipe, thinking I would recreate the beef patty and egg in a white muffin with a slice of American cheese. It's not where I ended up. Lentils and onions and veg gave way to a haggis-style patty, and the rest was history. For the 'cheese', I use either Follow Your Heart American Style slices, or Violife Cheddar-flavour slices. FYH are more authentically processed-tasting, whereas the Violife veers more towards firm cheese, so it depends on your palate. For the purposes of this recipe, I want filth and goo, but you may think otherwise. Serve in a white muffin, lightly toasted, with a generous dollop of ketchup.

---

1 Finely grate or very finely dice the onions, and wash and finely grate the carrots into a large mixing bowl. Grate the mushrooms, and peel and finely chop the garlic. If you have a small bullet blender or food processor, you can speed up this part simply by roughly choping the onion and garlic and halving the carrots, slinging them all in with the mushrooms and blitzing everything to smithereens.

2 Add all the vegetables to a large non-stick frying or sauté pan, and measure in the oil, nutmeg, allspice, salt and pepper. Cook on the smallest hob ring on a very low heat for 15 minutes, until the onion starts to soften but not brown at all, and stir intermittently to disturb it and prevent it sticking and burning.

3 Pour over the stock. Thoroughly rinse the lentils in a sieve or colander, under a cold tap, and add to the pan. Bring to the boil, then reduce to a simmer, and cook for 40 minutes until the lentils are very soft and swollen. Add the porridge oats, stuffing mix, sage and nutritional yeast, if using, and cook for 10 minutes more, stirring to combine. The oats and lentils will absorb the liquid so you may need to add a splash more, but too much will make the patty mixture too sloppy, so try not to go overboard.

$\longrightarrow$

Serves 4–6

---

2 large onions

2 large carrots

10 meaty mushrooms – chestnuts, shiitakes or baby portobellos

4 fat cloves of garlic

1 tbsp light cooking oil, plus extra for frying and greasing

½ tsp grated nutmeg

½ tsp ground allspice

A few pinches of salt and a generous grind of black pepper

220ml chicken-style or vegetable stock

75g dried red lentils

75g dried brown lentils

75g porridge oats

2–4 tbsp stuffing mix

1 tbsp chopped sage leaves

1 tbsp nutritional yeast (optional)

plain flour, for dusting

To serve

4 white muffins, sliced in half

8 slices of vegan 'cheese'

Tomato ketchup

4 When the porridge oats and stuffing mix are cooked and the mixture is thick, remove from the heat and tip into a mixing bowl. Allow to cool and then transfer to the fridge to firm up for an hour, or overnight.

5 When the mixture is cool and firm, remove it from the fridge. Heat a little oil in a non-stick frying or sauté pan. Break off a piece with lightly floured hands, the size of an average egg. Roll it in your hands to form a ball, adding a little more flour if it sticks to your palms. You want a patty the width of your muffin, and quite thin – this helps it to crisp up and cook through on both sides, and stops the dreaded 'soft middle' that vegetarian and vegan patties can fall victim to. You will be putting two patties in each muffin for the 'double muckmuffin' experience, so don't worry if they look a little flimsy at this stage.

6 If cooking for a crowd, preheat your oven to 160°C (fan 140°C/325°F/gas 3) and place a lightly greased baking tray on the middle shelf, and one on the shelf above. Fry each patty on a medium-high heat for 6 minutes on one side, and 4 minutes on the other. Remove and transfer to the oven, and repeat until all the mixture is used up.

7 Place your muffins on the top shelf of the oven for a few minutes to toast. Remove and assemble: bottom half of the muffin on the plate, patty, 'cheese', patty, 'cheese', ketchup, top half. Enjoy!

Tomato and Olive Scuffins

Makes 6 generously
proportioned scuffins

———————

3 tbsp cooking oil (sunflower
or vegetable), plus extra
for greasing

225g self-raising flour

2 tsp mixed dried herbs

2 tbsp strong grated vegan
'cheese' or nutritional yeast
flakes (optional)

1 x 400g tin of chopped
tomatoes

3 tbsp pitted black
or green olives, chopped

150ml vegan 'milk' (see intro)

Salt and black pepper,
to taste

———————

This is a scone made in a muffin tray, simply because at the time of writing this recipe I discovered a softer, tackier batter made for a better scone but was harder to roll out and cut up with a cookie cutter in the traditional manner. And so I dolloped it into a 6-hole greased muffin tray, and the Scuffin was born. Simply halve it and eat like an unconventionally shaped scone.

For milk, almost any plant-based equivalent works here. Coconut and almond are a little on the sweet side, but would do; soya, hemp, rice or cashew would be my recommendations, depending on what you like and generally use. I suppose the exception would be hazelnut, which might be ghastly with olives!

Cheese isn't essential, but for those of you who like a cheesy kick to your savoury baked goods, Violife mature Cheddar-flavour block or some nutritional yeast flakes would deliver this handsomely.

1 First preheat your oven to 200°C/400°F/gas 6, and lightly grease a deep 6-hole muffin tin. Set to one side for the moment.

2 Measure the flour into a large mixing bowl, and add the herbs, salt and pepper, and 'cheese' or nutritional yeast flakes, if using. Mix well to evenly distribute the dry ingredients.

3 Tip the tomatoes and oil into the mixing bowl. Add the olives and the 'milk', and mix well to form a thick batter.

4 Divide the batter evenly between the holes in the muffin tin, until each is two-thirds full, to allow room for expansion. Pop the scuffins in the oven for 18–22 minutes, or until risen and golden and a sharp knife inserted into the centre comes out clean.

5 Allow to cool for 10 minutes to firm up a little, then remove from the tins and serve. Keeps for 2–3 days in an airtight storage container or freezer bag. Freezes well too, but for best results, defrost completely before cooking, and reheat in the oven.

Chocolate Peanut Butter Spread

My Small Boy loves Nutella, and he would happily eat nothing else if given sole autonomy over his weekly diet. This recipe came about from trying to make my own, and realising that hazelnuts are expensive at the rate at which he consumes them, so I needed a wallet-friendly alternative. Reese's make a decent peanut butter chocolate spread, but it contains skimmed milk powder, so once again, it isn't vegan. This simple recipe can be made without a blender – I know I rely on mine quite heavily on weak-wristed days, as it's easier to fling it all in and let the machinery do the hard work, if you have one, but it's easy enough without.

Makes 1 x 400g jar

———————

400g smooth peanut butter

4 tbsp cooking oil

2 tbsp caster sugar

4 tbsp cocoa powder

———————

1 Spoon the peanut butter into a large mixing bowl. Add the cooking oil and caster sugar and beat together with a fork or wooden spoon to combine. Keep mixing until the sugar dissolves.

2 Add the cocoa powder and mix again to make a dark, glossy spread. Spoon into a clean jar, (ideally sterilized, see Tip on page 23) and seal tightly with the lid.

3 Standard Nutella doesn't need to be stored in the fridge, but I would recommend that you do so with this homemade version, for food safety reasons. It will keep for 2 weeks in the fridge; the contents may settle or split, and this is completely normal – just give it a quick stir with a knife to re-combine them before using.

Breakfast Wrap with Banana Chilli Ketchup

Serves 2

1 small onion or 3 spring onions, thinly sliced

1 tbsp cooking oil

400g mushrooms, sliced

A handful of greens, thinly sliced – kale, spinach, chard or spring greens work well

2 tortilla wraps

Salt and black pepper

For the banana chilli ketchup

4 bananas

4 fat cloves of garlic

100g sugar

100ml vinegar – cider, white wine, spirit or pickling

½ tsp chilli powder

1 tbsp mustard seeds

1 tsp nigella seeds (optional)

I first made this for breakfast while staying in a hotel in Edinburgh that turned out to be a self-catering apartment. It takes a certain amount of planning to buy exactly enough food to sustain two adults for three days, wasting nothing, when your only shopping options are the Harvey Nichols food hall (ineffectual, expensive, but fun to walk around gasping at), or a Sainsbury's Local, where fruit and veg are sold in large packets and nothing by the gram. I found a banana habanero chutney in Harvey Nicks by Mr Vikki's, a small Cumbrian company, and Louisa and I wolfed our way through two jars of it in a weekend.

I knew that as soon as I got home and into my own kitchen, I would be knocking up my own version. I put mine into a naan initially – an idea I owe to Dishoom, my all-time favourite restaurant, whose breakfast naans are the stuff of legend. This is basically a tribute to the best parts of my 31st birthday weekend away, in an edible format; without the need to scale a small mountain in the afternoon to burn it off. I feel it would be impetuous of me to swipe the breakfast naan from under their feet, especially as Dishoom have their own, beautiful cookbook, so I have served it here in a floury tortilla wrap, which is tremendously delicious.

1 First make your banana ketchup. Peel the bananas and break the chunks into a bowl, then mash them with a fork until well broken up and a bit sloppy. If you have a small bullet blender, pop them in – it makes seconds of work out of this and gives a smoother end result.

2 Transfer the bananas to a medium-sized saucepan, preferably a non-stick one or one with a heavy bottom. Peel and finely slice the garlic cloves and add them to the pan, along with the sugar, vinegar,

$\longrightarrow$

Vegan(ish)

chilli and mustard seeds and, if using, nigella seeds. Turn the heat up to medium and cook for a few minutes, stirring intermittently, until the banana mixture starts to spit at you. Impolite, I know, but that's how you know things are happening. Reduce the heat to low and cook for 30 minutes, or until the liquid has reduced by a third and thickened. Remove from the heat and pour into a clean (preferably sterilized, see Tip on page 23) jar. Seal and leave to cool before transferring to the fridge.

3 To make the breakfast wrap, toss the onions into a large non-stick frying or sauté pan. Add the oil and a pinch of salt and a little pepper, and cook on a low heat for 4–5 minutes until they start to soften. Add the mushrooms to the pan and cook for 5 minutes more, then add the greens and cook for a further minute until wilted.

4 Warm the tortillas in the microwave for 30 seconds, or 2 minutes in the oven at 180°C/350°F/gas 4 if you don't have a microwave. Remove. Spread thinly with banana ketchup. Add a generous pile of mushrooms, onions and greens. Fold the bottom third up, then roll up. Seal with extra ketchup and serve immediately.

Store leftover ketchup in a clean jar in the fridge and use within a month. It makes a great accompaniment to curries, lends a sweet spicy kick to hearty salads, and is delicious in a cheese sandwich – especially a grilled one

Vegan(ish)

Everyday Sausages

This is my favourite go-to vegan sausage recipe, and the title somewhat underplays their magnificence, as I would gladly eat these every single day. The filling also makes incredibly delicious sausage rolls, fooling all of my friends and family into thinking they are the real thing, which, in my mind, they absolutely are. I use Violife Original block for these — it's merely a binding agent though, so any faux Cheddar or mozzarella-style 'cheese' will do the same job. These sausages are ideal in a fry-up, piled atop some creamy mash, stuffed in a bread roll with lashings of brown sauce, ketchup or mustard, or simply enjoyed cold from the fridge.

Makes 20
(easily frozen)

1 x 400g packet cooked chestnuts

250g silken tofu

1 large onion, red or white

120g sage and onion stuffing mix

120g mild vegan 'cheese'

1 tbsp soy sauce

Plenty of black pepper

Oil, for greasing and frying

To serve (optional)
Grilled mushrooms
Grilled tomatoes
Baked beans
Steamed kale

1 Tip the chestnuts into a small bullet blender or food processor and pulse them to a fine crumb. Tip into a large mixing bowl and add the silken tofu.

2 Peel and finely chop the onion, as small as you can — you may find it easier to sling this in the food processor too, but I get a great deal of satisfaction out of pulverising vegetables with a large, heavy knife, although now I've committed that to print, I admit it looks a little unusual. Never mind. Add the onion to the bowl of chestnut crumb and tofu.

3 Add the stuffing mix, and grate in the 'cheese'. At this point, I return the entire lot to the blender in batches to create a fairly smooth sausage mix — this is not essential, but as the mother to a Small Boy who is increasingly fussy about 'bits' in his food (my eternal shame, as a food writer, is rearing a wilfully culinary-defiant progeny), I do it to save arguments in my household, and also, it makes for a superior sausage.

4 Return to the mixing bowl and add the soy sauce and plenty of black pepper. It needs no further seasoning; the sage and onion stuffing mix does all the heavy lifting on the flavour front and the soy sauce adds all the salty depth you need. Leave it to stand for 30 minutes so the stuffing can absorb the liquid and swell and

⟶

thicken. This is a good time to tackle washing the blender or food processor, as this mixture dries like cement.

5 When the mixture is firm, form it into sausage shapes. I have a method for this that is super simple and stops my hands getting too sticky. Grab a piece of baking parchment or greaseproof paper and cut it into a square. Fold this into nine equal pieces and cut those into squares (they should be roughly 13cm in size if you're using standard supermarket-sized paper). You will only need a couple of them, so store the rest somewhere safe – mine are in a freezer bag in the utensils drawer, marked 'sausage paper'.

6 Brush a little oil over a paper square with your fingertips. Dollop the sausage mix in the middle. Gently fold the paper in half, and roll it with your palm to fingertips and back again to form a very neat, compacted sausage shape. Pop it into a lightly greased airtight container, and repeat. When the paper starts to get too messy, discard it and use another piece.

7 Separate the sausages in layers in the container, using one of your helpful squares of sausage paper, lightly greased on each side, to stop them sticking together. Repeat until all the sausage mix has gone, or you have made as many sausages as you need, for the mixture will freeze well to be used at a future date.

8 Pop the sausages in the freezer for 15 minutes to set – this makes them easier to cook and stops them falling apart in the pan.

9 When set, place them in a non-stick frying pan with a little oil. Bring to a high heat, then reduce to medium. Cook for around 8 minutes, nudging them carefully every now and then to ensure they cook evenly. Unlike regular sausages, there's nothing in there that will harm you if eaten raw – they will just taste a little less fantastic.

10 Once cooked, serve hot. Or cold. Or however you please. They keep in the fridge for 2 days or in the freezer for a few months.

Two

Soups

'Chicken' Soup

Serves 2

————————

1 × 400g tin of baked beans

2 tsp chicken-style stock or powdered broth – I use Osem

1 large carrot

1 large onion

6 fat cloves of garlic

A generous grind of black pepper

A few handfuls of greens or a mix of greens and trimmed green beans

A dash of lemon juice

This is as close to a chicken soup as any vegetarian or vegan one could possibly come. The star of the show is the stock; a must for the base of any good soup recipe. There are now many vegan chicken-style stocks available, and my favourite is Osem Chicken Flavour Soup and Seasoning Mix. I originally wanted to make this soup with butter beans, for Mrs J, who requested them, but I left the pan unattended this morning and burned them to a smoky pungent crisp, so instead I found myself rummaging in the cupboard looking for a replacement. Behold, the baked bean, thoroughly rinsed of all its sticky orange sauce, and a worthy, and impossible-to-detect, substitute. Half the price, too. I added freshly picked chard from my garden (I keep meaning to write about that, because it is very simple to grow and almost impossible to kill).

————————

1 First thoroughly rinse your baked beans under running water in a sieve, to get rid of all of the sticky tomato sauce. They won't get completely clean, but any lingering sweetness will be absorbed into the soup as it cooks. Pop the beans into a medium saucepan.

2 Pour over 800ml cold water, add the stock powder and bring to a gentle simmer.

3 Finely slice your carrot – I don't bother to peel mine – and peel and slice your onion, and toss into the pan. Peel the garlic cloves and add those too. (You can, of course, use tinned carrots, frozen onions and lazy garlic paste, for a far simpler endeavour.)

4 Season generously with black pepper, and cook for 30 minutes on a gentle simmer. The soup may thicken as it cooks and as the beans break down, making it deliciously creamy, so keep your eye on it and add a splash of water if required.

5 To serve, toss in the greens and/or green beans 2 minutes before serving, and finish with a splash of lemon juice. The stock is plenty sufficient in salt, so it won't need any more of that, but a dash more black pepper to taste makes it extra warming and delicious.

Powdered chicken-flavour Osem is sold in large tubs in most supermarkets. If you can't find it with the stocks, it may be in the speciality ingredients aisle, as it is a kosher product

Vegan(ish)

French Onion Soup

Serves 4

———————

700g mixed onions

4 cloves of garlic

60g good buttery
vegan spread

1 tbsp flour

1 litre chicken-style stock –
I use Osem (see intro on
page 50)

1 tbsp red or white vinegar

1 tsp any kind of mustard

4–6 slices of bread

Oil, for roasting

Salt and black pepper,
to taste

A good onion soup is a classic recipe to have in your repertoire; ideal for autumn evenings and cold winter lunches, and knocked together with the simplest and cheapest of ingredients. I use this recipe as a baseline and often substitute half of the stock for ale or white or red wine, as the mood takes me. You can use any kind of onions here; be they red, white, green or spring, any onions will do.

———————

1 First peel and finely slice your onions and garlic; I admit to using a mandoline to make quick work of this, limiting the amount of time I spend sobbing into the kitchen worktop. These devices look intimidating but they make short work of tough vegetables – just mind your fingers and concentrate! If you don't have a mandoline, a sharp knife will do the job just as well.

2 Toss all of the onions and garlic into a large heavy-bottomed pan, preferably a non-stick one. Add the buttery spread and bring to a very low heat on the smallest hob ring. Sweat for 10 minutes to cook the onions very, very slowly – you don't want them to brown.

3 When 10 minutes have passed, stir in the flour, then add a third of the stock. Cook for 10 minutes more. Add the remaining stock, vinegar and mustard, and stir well. Bring to the boil, then reduce to a simmer and cook for 40 minutes more.

4 About 10 minutes before the soup is finished, preheat the oven to 160°C (fan 140°C/325°F/gas 3) and slice the bread into fingers, then dice each finger to make croutons. Toss them in a little oil, season with salt and pepper, and place on a baking tray. Pop into the oven for 8–10 minutes to toast.

5 Serve the soup piping hot, seasoned to taste with salt and plenty of pepper, and scattered with the croutons.

Vegan(ish)

Cannellini and Garlic Soup

This recipe is extremely simple but sustaining – solace in a deep bowl on a cold evening. You can make variations of it with whatever herbs you like; I find rosemary and thyme also work well, and basil in the summer. Don't scrimp on the garlic, as it holds it all together.

<hr>

1 Drain the cannellini beans keeping the liquid (for aquafaba, see page 12). Rinse the beans and add them to a large saucepan. Cover with stock, and bring to the boil – big, rolling bubbles. Reduce to a simmer and add the garlic. Cook for 45 minutes until soft and creamy.

2 Remove the beans with a slotted spoon and place them in a blender, then cover with the cooking liquid. Tip any cooking liquid that doesn't fit in the blender into a nearby bowl, mug or similar vessel – you may need it, but you need a clear pan to pour the soup back into.

3 Blend until smoothish, then pour back into the pan. Add the oil or spread and parsley, and taste it. Season with a little salt and pepper, and a dash of lemon juice or vinegar if you feel it needs it. Add some of the reserved cooking liquid and stir in until the soup reaches your desired consistency; some like it thick, some sippable, the preference is entirely personal.

4 Serve with plenty of black pepper and some nice bread to dunk in it.

Serves 2

<hr>

2 x 400g tins of cannellini beans

800ml chicken-style stock – I use Osem (see intro on page 50)

4 cloves of garlic or 2 tbsp garlic paste

2 tbsp cooking oil or vegan spread

A fistful of fresh parsley, chopped (optional)

Salt and black pepper, to taste

A dash of lemon juice or vinegar (optional)

Bread, to serve

Roast Tomato and Thyme Soup

Serves 2

———————

Cooking oil, for greasing

1kg fresh tomatoes

400ml vegetable stock or chicken-style stock – I use Osem (see intro on page 50)

1 tbsp vinegar – red, white or cider

A few sprigs of fresh thyme

Salt and black pepper, to taste

I make this soup with the cheapest of salad tomatoes from the supermarket or greengrocer, partly because the recipe calls for such a great quantity of them, and partly because I love the transformation from slightly hard, insipid, unloved tastelessness to deep scarlet and flavour-drenched, simply by popping them in the oven. I deliberately leave this soup very simple, unadorned to really appreciate the buttery smooth, rich taste of the tomatoes, scattered with a little thyme and black pepper. I cook my tomatoes for an hour, but the longer you can leave them, the better this gets.

———————

1 First heat your oven to 180°C (fan 160°C/350°F/gas 4) and very lightly grease a baking tray.

2 Halve your tomatoes and jostle them onto the tray – mine all fitted on one, but it was a bit of a squeeze! They shrink a little as they cook, as the juices evaporate, so don't worry if it looks a little busy. Cook in the centre of the oven for 30 minutes, then gently turn them over and cook for 30 minutes more.

3 When soft and slightly caramelised, remove from the oven and tip into a blender or food processor. Add the stock and vinegar, and blend until smooth.

4 Pour into a saucepan and cook over a low heat – you don't want to boil it. Add the thyme and simmer gently for 10 minutes to infuse. Season to taste with salt and pepper, remove the thyme sprigs and serve.

Vegan(ish)

Chickpea, Leek and Fennel Soup

When I first made this soup for myself, it was with a small bulb of fennel I had found cheaply in my local greengrocers. But fresh fennel bulbs are generally an expensive ingredient, so I have substituted it here with fennel seeds. Feel free to use the bulb if you want to, but the soup is just fine without. This hearty recipe is based on a classic Italian soup, from *Polpo*, written by my friend Russell Norman – a sage on all things edible and Italian, restaurateur, and author of the most beautiful cookery books I am lucky enough to own.

----

1 Drain the chickpeas reserving the liquid (for aquafaba, see page 12). Rinse them thoroughly, then tip them into a large saucepan. Pour over the stock or water, crumbling in the cubes if using them, and bring to the boil. Reduce to a simmer and cook for 25 minutes, until the chickpeas are very soft.

2 Peel and finely slice the onion, and finely slice the leek, discarding the tough outer layer and dark green end. Add both to the pot – Russell cooks them separately and adds them in later, but I'm lazier in the kitchen than he is and prefer to minimise my washing-up pile. Add to the pan, along with the fennel seeds, chilli and plenty of black pepper. Cook for 15 minutes more on a simmer, adding more liquid if required.

3 When the veg is very soft, remove a third of the veg and chickpeas from the pan with a slotted spoon and set to one side. Transfer the remaining soup to a blender and pulse until smooth. Tip back into the pan. Season with salt and pepper to taste.

4 Serve, topped with the reserved veg and chickpeas and a final smattering of black pepper.

Serves 2

----

1 x 400g tin of chickpeas

1 litre vegetable stock or chicken-style stock – I use Osem (see intro on page 50)

1 large onion

1 large leek

1 tsp fennel seeds

A pinch of chilli flakes or powder

Salt and black pepper, to taste

Cannellini Beans and Greens Soup

Serves 2

2 large onions

6 fat cloves of garlic

1 tbsp fresh rosemary leaves
or 1½ tsp dried

2 tbsp cooking oil

2 x 400g tins of cannellini or
haricot beans

600ml vegetable stock
or chicken-style stock –
I use Osem (see intro
on page 50)

150g greens
(spring greens, kale, green
cabbage, chard – anything)

1 tbsp lemon juice,
fresh or bottled

A generous grind of
black pepper

This recipe is a favourite for balancing out periods of indulgence; it is creamy and hearty, while also feeling light and healthy. To make more of a meal of it, pour it over cooked pasta, piling the beans and greens on top as the broth pools in the middle. If you have any stale bread kicking about, tear it up and fling it in.

1 First peel and finely slice your onions and toss them into a large saucepan. Peel and halve the garlic cloves, lengthways, and add those too. You can chop them up smaller if you like, but I like to find them as soft, sweet jewels hiding in my bowl of soup.

2 Finely chop the rosemary if using fresh stuff, and add it, or the dried rosemary to the pot. Drizzle over the oil, and bring to a low heat on a medium hob burner for 10 minutes to start to slowly sweat the onions. Don't be tempted to crank up the heat, or else the onions and garlic and herbs will burn and you will have to begin again.

3 Drain the cannellini or haricot beans, reserving the liquid (for aquafaba, see page 12). Thoroughly rinse the beans and tip them into the pot. Cover with the stock, bring to the boil, then reduce to a simmer and cook for 45 minutes, until the beans have thickened the soup.

4 Finely chop the greens and stir them through, along with the lemon juice and a generous amount of black pepper. Serve immediately, or warm through as required.

Vegan(ish)

Jerusalem Artichoke, Leek and White Bean Soup

This soup is an ideal way to use up Jerusalem artichokes, the small, knobbly and tempestuous little tuber with no relation to either the artichoke or Jerusalem. Eating large amounts of these veg can cause noisy side-effects, so it's best to make enough soup for the whole family and giggle at each other for the rest of the evening. This is light, delicate and very moreish, but one bowl is probably enough! Leftovers can be thickened as a pasta sauce simply by cooking pasta in it from cool, and allowing the starch to do the rest.

---

1 First peel and very finely slice the onion, and do the same with your leek from the white part at the bottom, up to the green, stripping and discarding tough green outer layers as you go. Transfer the onion and leek to a large heavy-bottomed saucepan with the oil and a pinch of salt and a little pepper. Cook on a very low heat for around 10 minutes to start to soften the onion and leek, but do not allow them to brown. Stir occasionally to prevent them from sticking or burning.

2 While the leeks and onions soften, gently scrub your artichokes. I keep a small nail brush beside the sink for cleaning vegetables – cheaper and simpler than a bulky vegetable brush.

3 Once peeled or cleaned, slice your artichokes and add to the pan. Cover with the stock, and bring to the boil. Reduce to a simmer and cook for 30 minutes on low – a long slow cook helps to break down the inulin in the artichokes (the carbohydrate that converts to carbon dioxide, aka noxious gas) so if you have a delicate constitution, it's worth not rushing this step. Drain and rinse the cannellini beans, reserving the liquid (for aquafaba, see page 12) and add to the pan with the lemon juice. Cook for 20 minutes more.

4 Transfer the soup to a blender and blend until smooth. Return to the pan. Add the 'milk' and warm through gently without bringing to the boil, otherwise the 'milk' will spoil. Season with pepper to taste, and serve.

Serves 4

---

1 large onion

1 large leek

2 tbsp cooking oil

650g Jerusalem artichokes

600ml vegetable stock or chicken-style stock – I use Osem (see intro on page 50)

1 x 400g tin of cannellini beans

1 tbsp lemon juice, fresh or bottled

400ml vegan 'milk' (soya or cashew works best here)

Salt and black pepper, to taste

If you really must peel the artichokes, do, but their unusual shape makes for a lot of effort and a lot of waste, so I give them a quick once over in a shallow sink of cold water instead

Cuban Black Bean Soup

Serves 2

—————

100g onions, red or white

2 garlic cloves

1 tsp ground cumin

1 tsp mixed dried herbs

Cooking oil, for frying

1 x 400g tin of black beans

1 x 400g tin of
red kidney beans

400ml vegetable stock

200g passata or
tinned tomatoes

1 tsp vinegar – any
clear kind

Salt and black pepper,
to taste

To serve

Dried chilli flakes

Lime juice

This recipe is inspired by one from *Heat*, by my dear friend and prolific food writer Kay Plunkett-Hogge. What Kay doesn't know about chillies frankly isn't worth knowing; and I turn to her tome regularly when looking for something to perk up a drizzly day or blast away a lingering cold. This was one such situation, and this spicy, protein-packed little number hits the spot every time. Kay's recipe is far better than my simplified version of it, for which I hope she will forgive me.

—————

1 First peel and finely slice your onions, and peel and mince your garlic, and toss them into a large heavy-bottomed saucepan with the cumin, herbs, and a splash of oil. Bring to a low-medium heat, and cook gently for 5 minutes to start to soften.

2 Drain and thoroughly rinse the black beans and kidney beans, and add them to the pot. Cover with stock, and bring to the boil. Don't salt it yet; some beans can be mighty stubborn about seizing if salted too soon. Boil vigorously for a minute, then reduce to a simmer. Add the passata or tomatoes and stir. Simmer for 40 minutes, until the beans are so soft that they are falling apart.

3 Take the pot off the heat, remove a third of the beans with a slotted spoon and set them to one side. Tip the remaining soup into a blender and pulse until smooth. Return it to the saucepan and pop it back on the heat for a moment, folding through the reserved whole beans. Add the vinegar, salt and pepper to taste, and thin with a little water or stock to your desired consistency.

4 Garnish with chilli flakes, a drizzle of lime juice and some extra black pepper, and serve hot.

Vegan(ish)

Mock-a-Leekie Soup

In years gone by, I used to celebrate Burns Night with friends, and raucous, unwieldy enthusiasm. I have no Scottish heritage (that I know of, and I did look desperately hard through my family tree willing it to be so), simply a love of poetry and hearty dinners. January is often the coldest month of the year, so what better excuse to eat soup and read aloud odes to lairds and lassies with some of my favourite people? It's a tradition I lost when I fell into poverty – not that chicken stock and canned prunes were particularly hard to come by, but reasons to be jovial were. I hope that my Scottish friends will forgive me this deviation, and turn a blind eye to the vegan haggis-style patties further buried within these pages. Some hae meat and canna eat, and I guess some of us just don't want it!

Serves 2, generously

———————

1 onion

2 medium leeks

2 carrots, washed and finely diced

1 large potato, scrubbed and finely diced

A a few sprigs of thyme or mixed dried herbs

A splash of white wine – not particularly essential but nice all the same

500ml vegetable stock or chicken-style stock – I use Osem (see intro on page 50)

10ish tinned or dried prunes, pitted and roughly chopped

Salt and black pepper, to taste

Bread, to serve (optional)

———————

1 Slice the onion and finely slice the white and pale green parts of the leek, discarding any dark tough outer leaves. You can freeze these and toss them in a stock pot further down the line, but they really are too tough for everyday cookery, even with hours of slow cooking. I know; I've tried it, and the results were, well, particularly gusty. Anyway, pop the onion, leeks and finely diced veg into a large pan and add the herbs.

2 Cover with the wine, if using, and stock. Bring to the boil and reduce to a simmer, then cook for 20 minutes until the vegetables are very soft.

3 Remove half of the veg with a slotted spoon and set to one side. Discard the sprigs of thyme, if using. Tip the soup carefully into a blender and blitz until smooth. Return it to the pan and add the veg. Season with salt, if required, and plenty of black pepper. Top with the prunes, and serve.

Three

Sandwiches

Tunha Sandwich

Makes enough filling
for 2 generously filled
rounds of sandwiches

───────────

1 x 400g tin of
haricot beans

2 spring onions or ½ onion

100g tinned sweetcorn

4 tbsp Vegan Mayo
(see page 81)

1 tbsp lemon juice

1 tbsp aonori (see intro)

A pinch of salt and
a generous grind of
black pepper

Bread rolls or slices of
bread, to serve

Credit for the name of this recipe must go to my dear friend and taste-tester, Caroline, who upon trying it couldn't work out how I'd done it and upon asking me, I replied with a triumphant 'ha!' and ran from the room with glee to fetch some more. It's not a direct replica of a tuna sandwich, but it's a pretty good replacement, and can be knocked up in a jiffy. Aonori is a kind of finely ground seaweed powder that can be found in higher-end supermarkets with the herbs and spices, Japanese food stores or online. It is useful for lending a fishy flavour to foods, and as well as being the seasoning for this sandwich, can be used with tofu to make 'fish' fingers, or in soups to make a deep, rich-flavoured base.

───────────

1 First drain and rinse your haricot beans and tip them into a large mixing bowl. Mash them to an absolute pulp with a fork or masher.

2 Finely chop the spring onions or finely dice the normal onion, and stir it through the mashed beans – this gives your basic flaky texture that a standard tuna sandwich would have. Add the sweetcorn and mix well.

3 Spoon in the mayo and lemon juice, and add the aonori and black pepper. Mix well to combine. Taste, and season with a little salt, pepper and aonori to your liking. Smother onto a bread roll or slice of bread, and devour.

Vegan(ish)

Classic 'Egg' Sandwich

I challenged myself to recreate my favourite egg sandwich – the Egg, Tomato & Salad Cream – as a vegan version. In the early days of our courtship, Mrs J and I would always buy a packet at the train station when we met and split it, one each, with a watermelon chaser. I've probably eaten around a hundred of them in my lifetime, so I knew exactly the flavour I was looking for with this. This recipe comes pretty close, and she loves it so much she requests it on a regular basis.

1 First drain your tofu and gently squeeze it over the sink to drain any excess juices. Slice it 1.5cm thick, then crumble each slice into a large mixing bowl.

2 Chop your onion very finely, then chop it some more, and add to the mixing bowl. Season with a generous pinch of salt and plenty of black pepper. Add the turmeric and nutritional yeast and mix well to combine to a crumbly yellowy mess.

3 Finely slice the tomatoes, if using, and add to the mix, along with the cress. Spoon in the vegan mayo and the mustard and mix well to coat the tofu-egg mixture evenly. Spread on one slice of bread, generously. Pop the other slice on top, then halve or quarter it as you prefer, and serve. The filling will keep overnight in an airtight container in the fridge – I wouldn't recommend making the sandwich a day in advance as it can go a bit soggy.

Makes 4 generous sandwiches

250g firm tofu

½ onion

Pinch of salt and lots of black pepper

½ tsp turmeric

2 tbsp nutritional yeast flakes

100g fresh tomatoes (optional)

Lots of cress

4 tbsp Vegan Mayo (see page 81)

½ tsp English mustard

2 slices of your favourite bread, per serving

The Jack Reuben

Makes 2

1 x 400g tin of jackfruit in brine – I like Summer Pride

1 cooked small red beetroot

1 tsp vinegar – any clear kind

1 tsp each of salt and black pepper

½ tsp smoked paprika

2 tbsp light cooking oil, plus extra for frying

For the dressing

1 tsp finely chopped dill pickle

1 tsp finely chopped onion

2 tbsp Vegan Mayo (see page 81)

2 tbsp ketchup

1 tsp horseradish, if available, or English mustard

A dash of hot sauce

To serve

2 bagels, sliced, or 4 slices rye bread

Sauerkraut

Dill pickles, thinly sliced

2 slices smoked vegan 'cheese'

I've eaten a lot of salt beef sandwiches in my life: fat heavy numbers from Baker Street cafes that I could barely get my sizeable jaw around, midnight bagels in taxis passing through Brick Lane, New York food trucks, and supermarket pretenders that didn't quite hit the spot but were better than not having one at all.

A sandwich chapter would not be complete without this, the undisputed king of all sandwiches, so I set about trying to create a vegan version that would be just as delicious in its own right, while staying as faithful as possible to the original. This took a few tries; I marinated in beer, in powdered mushroom stock, in dark hoppy ales and Bisto granules, before I decided to just let the flavours speak for themselves and stop trying to imitate the actual beef.

The result is crisp but tender, dry enough but with a juicy bite and a tangy, salty, peppery familiarity, something that's equally at home in a toasted white bagel as a hunk of dark, sweet rye bread.

1 First drain your jackfruit through a fine-mesh sieve. Squeeze the excess liquid using your hands to push it against the sieve, until the fruit feels fairly dry, then pop it into a large mixing bowl.

2 Finely grate the beetroot over the top. Add the vinegar, salt and pepper, paprika and oil. Break up the jackfruit with a fork or spoon into tiny shreds so the marinade soaks right in. Leave for an hour in the fridge.

3 Meanwhile, make your dressing. Place the dill pickle in a small bowl with the onion. Add the Vegan Mayo, ketchup, horseradish or mustard and hot sauce, and stir well to combine. Put it in the fridge until required.

⟶

4 When the jackfruit is well marinated, tip it into a large non-stick frying pan. I prefer to do mine in a wok, but that's because I like the space to shove it all around a bit. A normal frying pan will do just fine. Add a splash of oil and cook on a high heat for a few minutes until it starts to sizzle, then reduce to a medium heat and cook for 15–20 minutes more, stirring occasionally to disturb it. You want the jackfruit to be slightly crisp at some of its edges, with a dry-but-juicy texture to imitate the salt beef.

5 Toast your bread – whether a bagel or rye bread – lightly on both sides. Now you need to move quickly. Smother the base layer with your jackfruit. Pile it high. Add sauerkraut, pickles and 'cheese'. Top with dressing. Pop the other slice on top. Halve it if you please – I prefer not to. Devour, over a plate, to catch all that will inevitably plop out the other side as soon as you take a bite. If it's not leaking, it's not full enough. There is no gracious way to eat this, you just have to get on with it! And enjoy.

Coronation Chickpea Sandwich

A coronation chicken sandwich used to be one of my favourites as a teenager; my parents would buy the pre-mixed deli tubs of it from the supermarket and I would eat it straight from the tub. Here's my vegan take on the classic – just as comforting and sweetly spiced as the original.

Makes enough filling for 2 generously filled rounds of sandwiches

———————

1 x 400g tin of chickpeas

½ small red or white onion, or spring onion or shallot if you feel fancy

100g Vegan Mayo (see page 81)

4 tbsp mango chutney

1 tsp curry powder, as mild or as hot as you please

1 tbsp lemon juice, fresh or bottled

A pinch of salt and a good grind of black pepper

4 tbsp sultanas or raisins

2 slices of bread per serving

Salad leaves, to serve (optional)

———————

1 First drain the chickpeas, reserving the liquid (for aquafaba, see page 12) for future use. Rinse thoroughly, and transfer to a small saucepan. Cover with cold water, and place on a medium hob ring. Bring to the boil, then reduce to a simmer, for 20 minutes, until the chickpeas are very soft.

2 Meanwhile, make the coronation dressing. Very finely chop, or grate, the onion into tiny pieces. If you have a small bullet blender or food processor it will make the work of a moment out of this, but if you don't, a sharp knife or the large holes on a box grater will do just fine. Transfer the onion to a small mixing bowl.

3 Add the mayo, chutney and curry powder, and mix well to combine. Add the lemon juice a little at a time, beating well to incorporate it – do not add it all at once as you run the risk of the mayo splitting, although vegan mayo tends to be slightly more robust and less petulant than its traditional counterpart. Season with a pinch of salt and a generous grind of black pepper, and fold in the sultanas or raisins.

4 When the chickpeas have softened, remove from the heat and drain. If you want to be meticulous about it, pick out any skins that have loosened, for a smoother and more pleasant sandwich, but I rarely bother. Tip the chickpeas, still warm, into the dressing, and mix well to coat all over. Refrigerate to cool completely.

5 To serve, spread thickly on one slice of bread. Top with the other – adding salad leaves if you like for a little crunch – and halve. Serve immediately, or wrap the sandwich tightly and keep for up to 24 hours.

Nasu Dengaku Buns

Makes 2 generous buns

———————

4 tbsp white miso paste

2 tbsp Japanese rice wine vinegar

2 tbsp brown sugar

1 tbsp soy sauce

1 tsp freshly grated ginger

Oil, for greasing

1 large purple or black aubergine

1 tbsp sesame seeds

2 soft white bread rolls, sliced

To serve

Salad leaves

Pickles

Nasu dengaku is one of my favourite dishes to cook at home – simple, sweet, tangy and delicious, while still tasting fresh and healthy, it works well atop a pile of fluffy rice, cold as a salad, as a snack or, my favourite, stuffed into soft white bread rolls with a heap of salad and some pickles and devoured warm, sticky, sweet and indulgent. If you can't find rice wine vinegar in the supermarket, use half the amount of a light white wine vinegar instead.

———————

1 First make your glaze. Measure the miso, rice wine vinegar, sugar and soy sauce into a small bowl and beat well with a fork to combine. Add the ginger and set to one side.

2 Lightly grease a baking tray and heat your oven to 190°C (fan 170°C/375°F/gas 5). Cut your aubergine into slices around 8mm thick, and lay the slices on the baking tray. Brush generously with the glaze. Place the tray on the middle shelf of the oven and cook for 20 minutes.

3 Remove, and turn over the aubergine slices. Brush again with the glaze and top with a sprinkle of sesame seeds and return to the oven for 15 minutes.

4 Remove from the oven and pile into soft white bread rolls. Add salad leaves and pickles, and serve.

Vegan(ish)

White Bean, Artichoke and Onion Sandwich

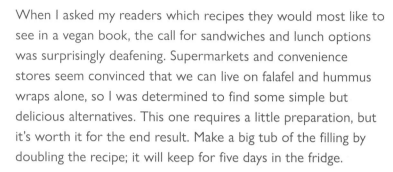

Makes enough filling
for 2 generously filled
rounds of sandwiches

———

1 x 400g tin of
cannellini beans

1 small onion

1 clove of garlic

4 tbsp sliced jarred
artichokes

1 tsp lemon juice or white/
red wine vinegar

3 tbsp Vegan Mayo
(see page 81)

Salt and black pepper,
to taste

4 slices of bread, to serve

When I asked my readers which recipes they would most like to see in a vegan book, the call for sandwiches and lunch options was surprisingly deafening. Supermarkets and convenience stores seem convinced that we can live on falafel and hummus wraps alone, so I was determined to find some simple but delicious alternatives. This one requires a little preparation, but it's worth it for the end result. Make a big tub of the filling by doubling the recipe; it will keep for five days in the fridge.

———

1 First drain and rinse your cannellini beans, reserving the liquid (for aquafaba, see page 12). Pop the beans into a small saucepan and cover with cold water. Bring to the boil, then reduce to a simmer for 20 minutes until super soft.

2 While the beans are cooking, peel and very finely dice the onion, and peel and mince the garlic. Transfer to a mixing bowl, along with the artichokes, and set to one side for now.

3 When the beans are soft, drain them thoroughly, and tip them into the bowl. Mash with a fork or masher to a rough paste, incorporating the onion, garlic and artichoke into the mixture. Add the lemon juice or vinegar and the vegan mayo, and mix thoroughly to combine.

4 Spread thickly on two slices of bread (I should recommend something wholesome like granary, but thick soft white bread is just so delicious), and top with two more. Halve, and serve.

The beans in the tin are already cooked, so if you are in a hurry you can skip step 1. I find they are slightly firm for my liking straight from the tin, but they may not be so for you. The best way to test is to pop a rinsed one in your mouth and see if it suits you

Vegan(ish)

BBQ Jackfruit Buns

A few years ago, pulled pork fashionably exploded onto the popular food scene — so ubiquitous that it is now rammed into sandwiches at supermarkets and on almost every pub menu. The vegan equivalent is almost indescernible from its porcine counterpart; soft, slow-cooked jackfruit takes on the flavours in the same way as slow-cooked pork does, but without the expense, nor the animal involvement. Heap this into buns hot or cold, or shape into burgers with a little flour and fry until crisp.

————————

1 First peel and finely slice the onion, and toss into a wide, shallow non-stick frying or sauté pan. Peel and mince the garlic, and add that too. Measure in the oil, and put the pan on the smallest hob ring on a low heat and soften the onion or garlic without browning. Cook for around 10 minutes. Add the spices, vinegar and passata, and stir well, before cranking up the heat to a medium flame.

2 Drain the jackfruit and lightly squeeze it in your hands to remove any excess liquid, then shred it so there are no large chunks. Add it to the pan with the sugar and soy sauce. Stir to cover with the sauce, and cook on a medium heat for 40 minutes, until the sauce has reduced and is pleasantly sticky. Serve piping hot, or cool and add to sandwiches and wraps.

Makes 4 generous buns
or sandwiches

————————

1 small onion

2 fat cloves of garlic

1 tbsp cooking oil

½ tsp ground cinnamon

½ tsp cumin, seeds
or ground

2 tsp paprika, sweet
or smoked

1 tbsp vinegar — red,
white or cider

400g passata

2 x 400g tins of jackfruit
in water or brine — I like
Summer Pride

1 tbsp sugar

1 tsp soy sauce

Buns, wraps, or bread,
to serve

Mock Duck Wraps

Serves 2

---

1 x 400g tin of jackfruit in brine – I like Summer Pride

1 tsp oil (sesame is best but any will do), plus extra for frying

½ tsp Chinese five spice powder

5 tbsp hoisin or teriyaki sauce

2 fat cloves of garlic, peeled and grated

2cm piece of fresh root ginger, peeled and grated

½ tsp Szechuan peppercorns, crushed

2 tbsp Vegan Mayo (see page 81)

2 floury tortilla wraps or 4–6 rice paper wraps, if available

½ cucumber, very finely sliced into matchsticks

A couple of spring onions, or a small amount of red or white onions, very finely sliced into thin strips

These are a riff on hoisin duck wraps sold in my local shop, which are themselves probably based on traditional Chinese crispy duck wraps from the takeaway over the road. So in the culinary world we do all borrow from one another, and translate our own experiences into slightly different recipes. Hoisin duck would traditionally be served in steamed buns, rice paper wraps or filo pastry spring rolls, so use those if you can. I have opted for the floury tortilla here as it is more widely available, and I hope more traditional tastes will forgive me for it.

---

1 Drain the jackfruit and squeeze firmly between your hands over the sink to squeeze out any excess liquid. Shred it into a mixing bowl with your fingertips, taking care to separate as much of the jackfruit as possible into small pieces.

2 In a small bowl, combine the oil, five spice powder and 3 tablespoons of hoisin or teriyaki sauce. Stir in the grated garlic, ginger and crushed peppercorns. Whisk well to combine the ingredients, then pour the mixture over the jackfruit. Mix well to coat, and allow it to marinate for an hour in the fridge. If you are in a rush, you can skip this step, but it does give a deeper, richer flavour as it permeates the whole fruit.

3 Add a splash of oil to a large frying pan or wok, and heat for a moment. Add the jackfruit and cook on a high heat for 5 minutes, then reduce the heat to low-medium and cook for a further 15 minutes, until the jackfruit has absorbed the liquid marinade and is quite dry looking. You want it almost crispy at the edges – if in doubt, taste a piece and cook for a little longer if required.

4 Combine the remaining 2 tablespoons hoisin or teriyaki sauce with the Vegan Mayo to make the sauce for the wraps. Spread over the wraps. Place the cucumber and onion strips in the centre of the wraps. Add the warm mock duck, then fold or roll up, sealing with a blob of hoisin mayo. Serve warm.

Vegan(ish)

The Big Jack

Makes 3 double burgers or
6 single burgers

75g white rice
1 small onion
1 small cooked beetroot
4 fat cloves of garlic
1 tbsp cooking oil,
plus extra for frying
200g mixed nuts
75g soya flakes
200g meaty mushrooms
– baby portobellos,
chestnuts or shiitake
40g vegan spread
1 tbsp soy sauce
A generous amount of
black pepper

For the sauce
1 small dill pickle or gherkin
3 tbsp Vegan Mayo
(see page 81)
2 tsp English mustard
1 tbsp tomato ketchup
A pinch of paprika
1 tsp white wine vinegar

To serve
Seeded hamburger buns,
sliced in half
Finely sliced red onion
Finely sliced lettuce
Slice of vegan 'cheese'
Sliced gherkin or dill pickle

Sometimes I am overcome with a sense of culinary mischief; a need to meddle in tried-and-tested popular dishes to see if I can recreate my own versions of them. This is one of those times. The usual disclaimer about it not being an exact replica applies; this is slightly more work than the original, and also it is made entirely from plants. If you're a stickler for absolute veganism, check the ingredients on your burger buns to make sure there are no traces of eggs or milk in them, as they can be a little sneaky. The proper 'special sauce' has onion powder and garlic powder in, but they're not ingredients I tend to keep in the house, so I left them out. If you have them or want them, add ½ teaspoon of each to the sauce.

1 First measure the rice into a small saucepan, and cover with double the volume of water. Bring to the boil, then reduce to a simmer. Cook for 20 minutes, until the rice is soft and the water has been absorbed.

2 While the rice is cooking, grate the onion and beetroot using the large round holes on a grater, and finely mince the garlic. Transfer to a non-stick frying or sauté pan, with 1 tablespoon of oil and a generous pinch of salt, and cook on a low heat for 15 minutes while the rice cooks, to soften.

3 Measure the nuts, soya flakes and mushrooms into a small bullet blender or food processor, and blitz to a breadcrumb consistency. Add the spread and half the rice, and blitz again. Tip into the mixing bowl with the remaining rice, add the soy sauce and black pepper, and mix well to evenly distribute. Transfer the mixture to the fridge to chill and firm for an hour.

$\longrightarrow$

Vegan(ish)

4 In the meantime, make the sauce. Very finely mince the dill pickle or gherkin into tiny, almost indiscernible pieces. Transfer to a small bowl. Add the mayo, mustard, ketchup and paprika, and stir to form a familiar-looking pale orange sauce. Add the vinegar a drop at a time, and stir in well – too much too soon and the sauce may split! Set aside in the fridge until needed.

5 When the patty mixture is firm, remove from the fridge. Break off a piece the size of a large egg, and roll in your hands to form a ball (roughly 150g in weight). Flatten it slightly, and set to one side. Repeat to make five more patties.

6 Heat a little oil in a non-stick frying or sauté pan. Add the patties one at a time, flattening gently until they are around 1cm thick, taking care not to let them crack at the edges. This may take a little practice! Cook for 6 minutes on one side, and 4 minutes on the other.

7 Assemble like so if you want to make double burgers: place the bottom of the bun on the plate. Spread a little sauce on the bun. Add onion, then lettuce, then 'cheese', then hot patty, then sliced pickles. Then add the second bun-bottom. Repeat as before: sauce, onion, lettuce, 'cheese', patty, pickles, and a dash more sauce for good measure. Top with bun top, and serve.

8 Retain the excess hamburger bun tops and blitz to use as breadcrumbs in cooking, baking, or for coating vegan nuggets in!

This method shows how to make double burgers, Big Jack-style, but you can easily adjust the recipe to make single burgers, including as many of the toppings as you like

Vegan(ish)

Vegan Mayo

Once you have a basic vegan mayo recipe, the possibilities are limitless. For garlic mayonnaise, simply add 1 tablespoon of garlic paste or ¾ tablespoon of freshly minced garlic. Or for a bright green and pungently sensational version, add a handful of wild garlic, finely chopped.

————————

1 Measure the aquafaba into the small cup compartment of a bullet blender.

2 Add the mustard, salt and pepper and blitz to combine. Add the vinegar and oil, and pulse for a minute, until the ingredients combine and emulsify to make a thick white mayonnaise. If it doesn't come together for you – and sometimes, it just doesn't – add ¼ teaspoon of xanthan gum and re-blend.

3 Store in a clean jar, preferably sterilized (see page 23), jar in the fridge for up to 2 weeks.

Makes 1 x 300ml jar

————————

3 tbsp aquafaba
(from cannellini beans,
see page 12)

1 tsp English mustard

1 tsp salt and generous
grind of black pepper

2 tbsp white wine or
cider vinegar

250ml sunflower oil

¼ tsp xanthan gum
(optional)

Four

Salad Bar

Raw Courgette Salad with 'Ricotta', Cannellini Beans and Preserved Lemon Dressing

Serves 2 as a side dish or
1 as a big lunch

————————

1 x 400g tin of
cannellini beans

A few big handfuls of
fresh lamb's lettuce or mixed
salad leaves

1 green courgette

1 yellow courgette
– or another green one
if you can't get hold of
a yellow

A few tbsp Vegan Ricotta
(see pages 98–9)

A few stalks of mint or
basil, leaves only

For the dressing
1 preserved lemon
1 fat clove of garlic
3 tbsp red wine vinegar
5 tbsp light cooking oil
A pinch of salt and a good
grind of black pepper

This simple salad is light and refreshing, ideal for a simple lunch or side dish, or can be extended into a larger meal by tossing with warm or cold pasta.

————————

1 First make your dressing. Finely mince the preserved lemon into tiny pieces, by slicing it thinly, then chopping the thin slices with a large, heavy chef's knife. Transfer to a small clean jar with a tight fitting lid. Grate in the garlic using the small holes on a box grater, or very finely slice it. Measure in the vinegar and then the oil, and season with a little salt and pepper. Screw on the lid and shake vigorously to emulsify and rough up the lemon and garlic.

2 Drain the cannellini beans, reserving the aquafaba (see page 12) and thoroughly rinse, then tip into a small mixing bowl. Douse with most of the preserved lemon dressing and toss well. Set to one side.

3 Line the bottom half of a serving bowl with a few generous handfuls of lamb's lettuce or mixed salad leaves. Top and tail the courgettes and using a vegetable or julienne peeler, peel the courgettes into fine, long strips from top to bottom.

4 Scatter the courgette on top of the salad leaves. Add the dressed beans. Dot with tablespoons of Vegan Ricotta, and finish with the remaining dressing, mint or basil leaves, and a generous grind of black pepper to serve.

Chickpea Caesar Salad

Serves 4

_____

1 x 400g tin of chickpeas

1 x 400g tin of jackfruit in brine or water – I like Summer Pride

Salt and black pepper

1 thick slice of bread

Oil, for brushing

2 tsp dried mixed herbs

1 head of lettuce – cos works well

For the dressing

2 cloves of garlic, peeled and minced

2 tbsp Vegan Mayo (see page 81)

1 tsp nutritional yeast flakes

½ tsp Dijon mustard

A dash of lemon juice

1 tbsp light cooking oil

Before I write this recipe, I owe something of an apology to my friend Jonathan. The first time we met, we were out for dinner with a large group of friends. Jonathan ordered the chicken Caesar salad, from a large and impressive menu, and I, nervous and slightly inebriated, subjected him to what is now affectionately known as The Caesar Salad Rant. Among other things, I dismissed the Caesar salad as unimaginative, barely a meal, not worth the money and more. I stand by my assessment of that particular dish, and its inclusion here is in no way a climbdown on my extremely strong feelings about a chicken Caesar salad. However, Caesar salads are classic for a reason, and a lot of people like them very much. Including Jonathan. So I made it my slightly petty mission to create a vegan Caesar salad that was imaginative, filling and absolutely worth a place on any restaurant menu. Here it is.

_____

1 First make your dressing. You'll need a decent-sized jar with a tight-fitting lid. Pop the minced garlic in the jar with the Vegan Mayo, nutritional yeast flakes, mustard and lemon juice. Season with a little salt and pepper, and stir well to combine. Add the oil and stir well to loosen the dressing. Add a tablespoon of cold water, and repeat. Screw the lid on the jar and shake it well to combine the ingredients, then set to one side until required.

2 Drain your chickpeas, reserving the aquafaba in a jar in the fridge (see page 12). Rinse them thoroughly, then tip into a large non-stick frying pan or sauté pan and fry for a few minutes until crisp.

3 Drain and thoroughly rinse the jackfruit, and press it in your palms to squeeze out any excess liquid. Break it up into a bowl, and season well with salt and a generous amount of black pepper. Add the crisp chickpeas. Toss with two-thirds of the dressing, and set to one side.

⟶

Vegan(ish)

4 Brush your bread with a little oil on both sides, and season with salt and pepper, and a sprinkle of mixed herbs. Dice and bake in the centre of the oven at 180°C (fan 160°C/350°F/gas 4) for 5 minutes to lightly toast, shaking halfway through, or dice and toss in a frying pan on a medium heat for a couple of minutes. Remove from the oven and set to one side.

5 Slice your lettuce and pop it into a large mixing bowl. Add the chickpeas and jackfruit and toss well to combine. Serve topped with the croutons and extra dressing.

Vegan(ish)

Salad Dressing Base

Everyone should have a basic salad dressing in their culinary arsenal, because once you know the formula, there are thousands of combinations and opportunities to experiment with.

Makes 1 small jar

7 tbsp oil – I use sunflower, you may wish to use a light olive oil instead but I honestly don't think it matters

5 tbsp white wine or cider vinegar

½ tsp salt

───────

1 Pour the oil and vinegar into a clean jar, preferably sterilized (see page 23), with a tight-fitting lid. Add the salt and screw the lid on.

2 Shake well to emulsify – when the two clear liquids combine to make a cloudy liquid, because science is fantastic. Remove the lid and taste a little of it. If it's too tangy for your liking, add more oil. If it's too slippery, add more vinegar. And that's it. It will keep for up to 2 weeks in the fridge.

Green and White Bean Pasta Salad

Serves 4

—————

200g small pasta shapes

200g green beans, fresh or frozen

150g petits pois, fresh or frozen

1 x 400g tin of cannellini beans

A few handfuls of kale or spinach leaves

For the dressing

2 fat cloves of garlic

3 tbsp light cooking oil

2 tbsp lemon juice, bottled or fresh

¼ tsp paprika

A pinch of salt and a good grind of black pepper

A handful of fresh mint or basil leaves

This delicious, protein-packed dish is ideal warm or cold, making it perfect for porting about to work or play. Enjoy for lunch or as an al fresco dinner on a summer's evening.

—————

1 Bring a medium-sized pan of salted water to the boil. Add the pasta and reduce to a simmer. Cook according to the packet instructions, usually 8–10 minutes, until soft but not falling apart. Halfway through, add the green beans and peas to the pan. Drain the cannellini beans, reserving the liquid (for aquafaba, see page 12), and add to the pan along with the peas and green beans.

2 Meanwhile, make the dressing. Peel and finely mince the garlic and transfer it to a small jar with a tight-fitting lid. Measure over the oil, lemon juice and paprika, and season with salt and pepper. Chop a quarter of the herbs and add to the jar. Screw the lid on tightly and shake well to combine.

3 When the pasta, beans and peas are cooked, drain and toss with the kale or spinach. Add the remaining mint or basil, and tip into a large serving bowl. Pour over the dressing, tipping in all the herbs and garlic, and toss to coat everything evenly.

4 Finish with extra black pepper and serve warm or cold.

Vegan(ish)

Beetroot Pickled Chickpeas

I made these as a lighter side dish to my 'Pork Belly' (see pages 172–5) for a group of friends for a special dinner. I wanted it to be a showstopper; something that would look beautiful and taste astounding – simple flavours but an absolute mouth party to boot. I love a pickle on the side of almost any savoury dish; the tang and brightness balancing the flavours of anything particularly heavy, or potent. I first made pickled beans in *Tin Can Cook*, from a Sarah Raven recipe, and I have several varieties under my ever-expanding belt now. These are my favourites – for their colour, their tenderness, their gentle sweet acidity – and they are the talking point at the dinner table. Every time I make a larger and larger jar of them, and every time, there is not a single one left.

---

1 Drain the chickpeas, and pop them into a large saucepan. Peel and finely dice the onions and add to the pan, and peel and slice the garlic and add this too.

2 Strain the vinegar from the jars of beetroot into the pan over the chickpeas. (You don't use the beetroot for this recipe, so refill the jars with half vinegar, half water to continue to preserve the beetroots and put the jars in the fridge for another day.)

3 Pour the 700ml vinegar over the chickpeas followed by the oil, sugar and salt. Bring to the boil, keeping a close eye on it as you are dealing with hot oil which, if left unattended, can pose a fire hazard. As soon as bubbles start to form, remove the pan from the heat immediately.

4 Allow the mixture to cool for a minute, stirring well, then divide the whole lot between two large sterilized jars (see page 23). Screw the lids on tight and leave to cool completely, before placing in the fridge. They are best if left for a week before sampling, without opening, as the flavours really start to sing, and only get better with time. They will keep for a few months, unopened. Once opened, use within a week.

Makes 2 x 800ml jars – keep one and give one away!

---

3 x 400g tins of chickpeas (720g drained weight)

2 large onions, red or white

1 whole head of garlic

Pickling vinegar from 2 x 100g jars of beetroot in vinegar

700ml vinegar – pickling, red wine or white wine

200ml oil – I use sunflower, feel free to use something 'better'

4 tbsp sugar

1 tbsp salt

I find it easiest to spoon the chickpeas between the two jars with a dessertspoon, then pour the liquid over the top to cover them

Potato Salad with Herb Vinaigrette Dressing

Serves 4

700g potatoes – I like new potatoes but it works with any you have to hand

1 tbsp lemon juice

A generous pinch of salt

2 spring onions

For the dressing

100ml light cooking oil

2 garlic cloves

5 tbsp red or white vinegar

1½ tbsp lemon juice

A pinch of salt and a generous grind of black pepper

A generous fistful of mixed fresh herbs – I recommend any combination of parsley, basil, mint, chives, coriander

A good potato salad is a staple on my lunch table when I have friends and family to visit, and this one is so popular it is affectionately nicknamed 'crack potato salad' by several of my friends! When Mrs J first took me to meet her friends – a momentous occasion for both of us, made all the more nerve-wracking by the fact they were hosting 'a lesbian Olympics' in Victoria Park for the afternoon. I armed myself with a large container of this potato salad, reasoning that what I lacked in confidence I could supplement with carbohydrates, and after an afternoon of running around with tights on our heads, trying to drop a biro into a wine bottle from our, er, butt cheeks and other high jinks, I whipped out my prize. The girls have been asking for the recipe for almost two years now, so here you go, enjoy!

1 First scrub your potatoes clean, but do not peel them; a lot of goodness resides just beneath the skin and it makes for a more flavourful dish to keep it on, as well as being simpler to prepare. Slice them thickly, then dice the slices and pop into a large pan of water. Add the lemon juice to the water to prevent the potatoes from discolouring, and a generous pinch of salt. Bring to the boil, then reduce to a simmer, and cook for 20 minutes, until the potatoes are tender. Finely chop the spring onions and set to one side for a moment.

2 While the potatoes are cooking, assemble the dressing. Measure the oil into a clean jar with a tight-fitting lid. Mince or slice the garlic and add it to the oil, then pour over the vinegar and lemon juice. Add the salt and a generous grind of black pepper, screw the lid on tight, and shake well to combine and emulsify.

Vegan(ish)

3 Chop the herbs, stalks and all, very finely, and add to the jar. Shake again to combine — if you have a small bullet blender, you can stuff everything into it and blitz it to a smooth green glossy oil, but I prefer the individual flavours of the different herbs to sing through, even though it is a touch more work.

4 When the potatoes are tender, drain them and toss with the dressing, to taste. Scatter the spring onions on top, and finish with extra black pepper. Serve warm, or chill in the fridge until needed. Any surplus dressing will keep in the fridge for 5 days or the freezer for a few weeks, and can be used as a cooking oil or marinade, or tossed through pasta.

Cauli, Ginger, Lentil and Lemon Salad

Serves 2 as a side or
1 very generously

½ head of cauliflower

1 × 400g tin of green lentils

A generous handful of
kale or chard – tough stalks
removed – or spinach leaves

For the dressing

2cm piece of fresh root
ginger, peeled and grated

2 fat cloves of garlic, peeled
and minced or grated

1 small preserved lemon
(optional, add 1 tsp extra
lemon juice if unavailable)

3 tbsp light cooking oil

1 tbsp lemon juice,
fresh or bottled

Salt and black pepper,
to taste

To serve (optional)

Seeds of 1 pomegranate

Green olives, roughly
chopped

1 tbsp sun-dried tomatoes
in oil, drained and roughly
chopped

This simple, hearty salad takes just minutes to knock together and only improves by being left to sit in the fridge overnight so that the flavours really develop, making it ideal to throw together in the evening and take to work the next day. Kale is more robust if you want to leave this overnight, but spinach works well too. You can improvise with accoutrements; this is delicious with fresh herbs added, slow-roasted tomatoes, pomegranate seeds, finely chopped olives, toasted chopped nuts – or whatever takes your fancy.

---

1 First make your salad dressing. Add the ginger and garlic to a clean small jar with a tight-fitting screwtop lid. Finely slice the preserved lemon, if using, and add that in too. Measure the cooking oil and lemon juice into the jar, and season with a little salt and a generous amount of black pepper. Screw the lid on and shake vigorously to combine and emulsify.

2 Chop the cauliflower into large florets and pop it into a small bullet blender or food processor until you reach a couscous-like texture. (You may have to do this in batches.) If you don't have a suitable food processor, you can grate it with the large holes on a box grater, starting with the stem side, and watching your fingers! Transfer the grated cauliflower to a large mixing bowl. Drain and thoroughly rinse the lentils and add them to the cauliflower.

3 Finely chop the greens and add to the bowl, then mix everything together thoroughly. Pour over the dressing, and finish with a generous grind of pepper (yes, another one). Serve immediately with extra toppings, if using, or chill until required. It will keep in the fridge, covered, for 2 days, and only improves with a little rest, as do we all.

Vegan(ish)

Garlicky Broad Bean Puree with Salad Leaves

Serves 2

_____

200g fresh or tinned broad beans – this is the podded weight, if using fresh

4 fat cloves of garlic, or adjust to taste

2 tbsp light cooking oil

1 tbsp lemon juice

A bag of salad leaves or herbs

Salt and black pepper

The humble broad bean can be a divisive ingredient; when I posted a photo of a brown paper bag of these glorious green goddesses on my Instagram account, around a quarter of the comments I received were from haters, and I must admit, I used to be one of them. As a child, I was occasionally served broad beans, cooked in chewy, barely digestible pods, and it took me until well into adulthood to even go near them again. And then I discovered 'double-podding'. Not just slipping them from their blankety beds with a deftly-applied flick of a well-exercised thumb, but also removing that thick, barely penetrable, greyish skin to reveal a nub of the brightest green, as round and fresh and delectable as the most petit of peas. This, dear reader, changed everything. Now, double-podding broad beans is a slow process, so do it in front of the telly, or when you have a little end-of-day stress to work out with a small sharp knife and a few minutes of patience.

If you lack the latter, you can substitute them with a mixture of tinned white beans and a shake of frozen peas, but don't knock it until you've tried it, for even the most hardened broad-despiser may change their minds on discovering that it's what's on the inside that counts. I folded through a sad bag of salad that I found for 9p in the reduced chiller of my local supermarket, but any herbs or leaves will do. You could even treat yourself and use fresh ones that aren't blackening around the edges, but if you have those kind of riches kicking around, you should probably be signed up to my Patreon ;-)

_____

Vegan(ish)

1 If using fresh broad beans, they will first need to be podded. I find the easiest way to do this is to twist the pods hard in the middle then 'pop' the beans out, but everyone finds their own rhythm with tasks like this. Try a few bashes, smashes and slashes and see what works for you.

2 Next, halve each bean lengthways to create two wide, flat beans, and peel away the white leathery skin. Discard it; I pop mine in the local food waste bin, but they can be ground up and folded through compost along with the pods, for extra goodness in the soil, if you are into that kind of thing.

3 If using tinned broad beans, simply open the tin, drain and rinse them, and laugh at how simple it was.

4 Pop the naked beans into a small pan and cover with cold water. Bring to the boil and reduce to a simmer. Peel and finely slice the garlic and add that too. Simmer gently for around 20 minutes, until the beans are super-soft and falling apart around the edges. Turn the heat up again and reduce the liquid down to barely anything at all, keeping an eye on it and stirring occasionally to prevent it sticking and burning and spoiling all of your hard work.

5 Remove the beans from the heat and mash well with a fork or masher, to form a rough paste. Add the oil and lemon juice and stir through. Season with salt and pepper, to taste.

6 Chop the salad leaves or herbs to smithereens with a large, heavy knife. My wrists are weakened with arthritis more days than not nowadays, so I confess to using a small bullet blender for this job now, but for many years a simple chef's knife and some perseverance did the job just fine.

7 Stir the leaves through the puree for a peppery kick and an instant hit of easy goodness. Use as a dip for chips, pitta breads or flatbreads, or serve with small steamed potatoes.

Vegan Ricotta

Makes 1 small jar

280g extra-firm tofu – I use
Naked by The Tofoo Co.

1 tsp lemon juice,
fresh or bottled

1 fat clove of garlic

1 tbsp nutritional yeast

A handful of mint or
basil leaves

½ tsp salt

A good grind of
black pepper

1 tbsp cooking oil

This recipe takes just minutes to knock together and makes a
great addition to salads, pasta, crackers and anywhere you would
use a standard ricotta. I vary the herbs according to the season
and the dish, interchanging them with coriander, parsley and mint
depending on my mood and what's available.

1 Add the tofu, lemon juice, garlic, yeast and herbs to a small
bullet blender or food processor and blitz to a paste. Season with
salt and pepper and stir in the oil.

2 Transfer to a clean jar (preferably sterile, see page 23) with a
tight-fitting lid, and store in the fridge with a splash more oil to
seal and preserve it for up to 3 days – any longer and it starts to
get a little funky.

Vegan(ish)

Artichoke, Bread and Tomato Dip

Makes 300ml dip

———————

2 slices of white bread

100g artichokes in oil

100ml oil – use the oil
from the jar of artichokes
and top up

2 tbsp lemon juice

2 tbsp tomato puree

Salt and black pepper

This recipe can be extended to make a soup or pasta sauce simply with the addition of vegetable or chicken-style stock, if you have no cause for a dip. Artichokes may seem like a fancy ingredient, but they are available cheaply from the supermarket stored in oil, usually sliced. I reserve the oil and use it here, or as a salad dressing, or for toasting rice in risotto – it is full of flavour.

———————

1 First pulverise the bread in a small bullet blender or food processor. Add the artichokes, oil and lemon juice, and blitz to a chunky paste – you don't want it to be completely smooth, unless that's your thing, but for me the texture is part of the appeal.

2 Remove from the blender and transfer to a bowl. Add the tomato puree and stir well to combine, adding a little more to taste if required. Season to taste with salt and pepper, and serve immediately, or chill in the fridge.

To use this as a pasta sauce, thin with 300ml chicken-style or vegetable stock and pour over cooked pasta

Vegan(ish)

Vegan Labneh

Labneh is a soft and creamy cheese that's popular in Middle Eastern cookery, and can be spiced with all manner of flavours. It is often served with honey, which I have substituted for golden syrup here; the contrasting sweet and sour tang is a very pleasing one. Dollop it on salads, eat it with flatbreads, or serve as a cooler beside spicy stews.

Makes 400g

300g plain soya 'yoghurt'

200g coconut 'yoghurt'

2 tbsp olive oil

2 tsp golden syrup

1 tbsp za'atar

Salt and black pepper

---

1 Line a sieve with a clean cloth (woven not fluffy – muslin, handkerchief or cotton are best). Place the sieve over a bowl or pan. Tip in the 'yoghurts' and twist the hanky like a sack at the top. Place a side plate on top and pop a tin of beans on it to weigh it down. Leave it for 24 hours in the fridge to strain.

2 About 24 hours later, tip/scrape the strained 'yoghurt' into a clean bowl. Season with salt and pepper and mix in half the oil and golden syrup – it will split, but it will come back together. Drizzle the remaining oil and golden syrup on top and sprinkle with the za'atar.

Five

Pasta, Rice and Noodles

Kindanara

Serves 4

———————

4 cloves of garlic

1 small white onion

2 tbsp plain flour

500ml vegan 'milk' – in order
of preference: cashew,
soya or rice

1 tbsp nutritional yeast flakes

1 tbsp cooking oil

300g spaghetti, tagliatelle or
linguine

4 tbsp sun-dried tomatoes
in oil

200g wild or shiitake
mushrooms

Salt and black pepper

A traditional carbonara recipe contains eggs, milk and bacon, and it was a challenge to recreate this, but I don't give up easily. I started off with technicalities – smoking thin strips of aubergine to replace the bacon, whisking aquafaba to give the unctuous richness of an egg – and it was delicious, but the ingredient list was as long as my arm. So I shelved that version, and instead of focusing on trying to replicate a carbonara, I came up with this kinder, kinda one instead. The oil, nutritional yeast and liquidized onion do all the heavy lifting in making a thick, creamy, flavourful sauce, and the sun-dried tomatoes and mushrooms give the meaty texture and deep, rich flavours. It's not a carbonara, but it is deliciously satisfying. And that'll do me just fine.

———————

1 First peel and finely slice the garlic cloves, and peel and slice the onion. Toss them into the blender, along with the flour, 'milk', nutritional yeast, oil, salt and pepper. Blend to a smooth liquid.

2 Pour the liquid into a saucepan and bring to a very low heat to cook and thicken. Cook for 15 minutes on low to knock out the ascerbic raw taste of the onion and garlic, stirring intermittently to prevent it from sticking and burning.

3 Meanwhile, pop the pasta in a large, wide pan of generously salted water and bring it to the boil. Reduce to a simmer and cook for 8 minutes or according to the packet instructions – tagliatelle may take a little longer than linguine.

4 While the pasta and sauce cook, drain and finely chop the sun-dried tomatoes and finely slice the mushrooms and add them to the sauce.

5 When the pasta is cooked, drain it and return it to the pan. Pour over the sauce and stir briefly to combine. Season generously with pepper and serve.

It is so much simpler to make the sauce in a small bullet blender, if you have one. It cuts out the usual laborious task of making a roux, then thinning it to a white sauce and praying for no lumps to materialize

Vegan(ish)

Come-to-bed Parmigiana

Serves 2

———————

1 large aubergine

4 fat cloves of garlic (you're both having it, it's fine)

2 tbsp light cooking oil, plus 1 tbsp

A few generous pinches of salt

1 x 400g tin of tomatoes

250ml vegetable stock

50g sun-dried tomatoes (optional)

200g dried spaghetti

1 tsp red wine vinegar or other vinegar

To serve

A pinch of dried chilli

A few small leaves of basil

A little black pepper

One day back in early 2017, I turned up to work late, sleepless, an incoherent babbling wreck chewed up by an 18-month landmark court trial and with bright copper dye fading from my wiry, tousled mania of hair. I left my walking stick in the lobby and limped in to work … to find a hand thrust towards me in a polite gesture of welcome, a smile, a curt hello. She introduced herself. I apologised seven times for my lateness and my pulled-from-a-car-wreck appearance. She was firm and professional, and she smiled at me again. And I felt that self-same car wreck collide with my solar plexus and toss me down a rabbit hole of giddy head-spinning highs and that soaring, almost nauseatingly disorienting feeling of time stopping and slowing and turning on its head. I stumbled away, a new crush ablaze across my cheeks and in every tip of my fingers, burning coiled springs in the soles of my feet, a song whispering in the cold, grey, slumbering chamber of my strange little heart. And then I went home and did what any self-respecting twenty-first-century romantic heroine would do; I followed her on Twitter.

Fast-forward a few weeks and, having established that my paramour was mutually curious, I found myself standing frozen in my kitchen, petrified, with a wooden spoon in my hand, wondering what to cook for her imminent arrival. I settled on this, and it has become synonymous, to me, with falling in love. It is not flashy, nor expensive; no grand gestures required. It requires a little patience, but very simple ingredients. It is homely, comforting, nourishing, the culinary equivalent of a soft warm body wrapped around your own. It delights, it satisfies, both firm and tender, messy and irreverent, hot and saline and sticky and sweet, and so much more than the sum of its parts.

It took her a month to pluck up the courage to tell me she doesn't like pasta, but I love her regardless.

———————→

Vegan(ish)

1 Finely slice the aubergine and toss it into a large, wide pan. Chuck in the whole peeled garlic cloves. Add the oil and salt and cook on a high heat for 5 minutes, turning or stirring intermittently to disturb the aubergines and stop them sticking to the pan.

2 Tip in the tomatoes, and add half the stock, and stir well. Bring to the boil briefly, then reduce to a simmer for 15 minutes, until the aubergine is soft, translucent and falling apart. This is a clumsy romantic metaphor. You're welcome.

3 Transfer the sauce to a blender, add the sun-dried toms, if using, and blitz it until smooth-ish. Add some more stock if you need to – the consistency should be that of cheap ketchup – and set to one side.

4 Rinse your pan under the tap to get the worst of the sauce off, and then pop the spaghetti in and cover it with water. Add a generous pinch of salt and any remaining stock. Bring to the boil and reduce to a simmer for 8–10 minutes until the pasta is *al dente*. Drain it and return it to the heat, stirring in the sauce, the vinegar and an extra tablespoon of oil, and crank it up high until it hisses and sizzles at you. Remove it from the heat quickly, top with a smattering of chilli, a kiss of basil and a twist of pepper, and serve.

Vegan(ish)

You-won't-believe-it's-vegan Bolognese

This recipe uses a little of a magic jar of dust I keep on my kitchen spice shelf – a long, pale-pink shelf stretching from one side of the kitchen to the other, organised in alphabetical order, as that's the fastest way to both find anything in a hurry and intimidate any interlopers into not trying to cook in my kitchen.

Nestled between the nigella and the mustard is a squat, wide round jar, scrawled upon with a Sharpie: 'Magic Dust'. Until now I have kept its contents a secret, adding it to lasagnes, Bologneses, gravy and anything that requires a hefty, beefy depth without the actual beef. It's simply dried mushrooms, many many of them, ground to a fine powder in a small bullet blender and passed through a sieve. Any pieces that remain in the sieve, too large to make the cut, are mixed with salt to make a mushroom salt that is delicious scattered on hot chips, or blended again, if you have the inclination, but after a while it becomes futile to even try. This is such a useful ingredient, and fast becoming a staple in my vegan cookery, that I keep my eyes peeled for reduced mushrooms in the supermarket and buy as many as I can carry, to dry out in the oven or open air and pulverize. It may seem a little pretentious, but a little goes a long, long way. If you don't have any dried mushrooms, you can substitute this with a tablespoon of red Bisto granules – it's not quite the same, but it yields a similarly delicious end result.

Serves 2, generously

400ml chicken-style stock – I like Osem

1 tbsp light soy sauce – reduce to 1 tsp if using lentils in place of soya flakes

150g dried soya flakes, or 1 x 400g tin of brown lentils

1 large onion, red or white

1 tbsp cooking oil

A pinch of salt and a good grind of black pepper

6 fat cloves of garlic

250ml red wine

2 tbsp tomato puree

1 tbsp mixed dried herbs

1 tbsp dried mushroom powder (see intro)

---

1 First make up your stock in a measuring jug or bowl, and add the soy sauce. Measure in the soya flakes and stir well, then leave them to one side to soak up the liquid. If using lentils instead, drain and rinse them and set to one side. You will need these presently.

⟶

2 Peel and finely dice your onion, and toss it into a large saucepan, preferably one with a non-stick base. Measure in the oil and add a pinch of salt and a good grind of pepper. Peel the garlic cloves and quarter them lengthways, and add to the pot. Cook on a low heat for a few minutes, stirring occasionally to prevent the onions and garlic sticking and burning.

3 Pour in the swollen soya flakes (or lentils), reserving some of the stock. Pour over the wine and add the tomato puree. Measure in the herbs and mushroom powder. Bring the pan to the boil, then reduce to a simmer. Simmer on a low heat for 30 minutes, until the liquid is greatly reduced and the sauce has thickened.
If the Bolognese gets too dry, add a little of the reserved stock.

4 Season to taste, and serve hot.

Vegan(ish)

Risotto Milanese (sort of)

Serves 4

---

1 large onion,
preferably white

3 tbsp olive oil, plus
extra for drizzling

1 litre vegetable or
chicken-style stock
– I use Osem

½ tsp saffron strands
(optional, because of
the expense, but
begrudgingly so)

350g risotto rice – usually
I would say long grain is
fine, but I'm tinkering
with enough here

150ml white wine

2 tbsp nutritional
yeast flakes

2 tbsp grated vegan
hard 'cheese'

My heaving shelf of Italian cookbooks informs me almost unanimously that in order to make an authentic risotto Milanese, you should start the stock with beef bone marrow first. That proved to be something of an insurmountable issue in a vegan recipe book, although given enough determination, some Bisto granules and some agar jelly, I'm fairly sure I could make a passable equivalent. I pondered long and hard about calling this Milanese at all, given that this version riffs on two of the most important ingredients: Parmesan and good meaty stock, and I have the greatest love for Italian food and all the parts of the beautiful country I have been lucky enough to visit so far. But no other recipe title seemed to encapsulate what I was doing quite as well as the original, so I've stuck with it, in the hope that I am forgiven. Remember, this is not the traditional method. It's my vegan take on it. For a true Milanese, seek out Giancarlo Morelli's recipe, or *Two Greedy Italians* by Antonio Carluccio and Gennaro Contaldo, or hop on over there and discover it for yourself.

---

1 Finely slice your onion, and toss it into a wide, shallow, non-stick pan. Add the vegan spread (or olive oil, if you can spare it). Cook on a low heat for 10 minutes, stirring occasionally to prevent the onions from sticking and burning. You want them super-soft and translucent, without a trace of browning on them, so settle in, this is going to be a recipe that requires patience as its key ingredient.

2 While the onions are softening, heat your stock, and add the saffron strands, so that they start to release their vivid yellow colour, and you get the most bang for your buck out of a comparatively expensive ingredient. Set to one side to infuse.

Vegan(ish)

3 When the onions have softened slightly, add the rice to the pan. Splash in a little of the saffron-infused stock, around 100ml, and turn up the heat. When it is almost all absorbed, pour in the wine and stir well. Turn the heat back down to low again. Add more of the stock, 100ml at a time, letting it mostly absorb into the rice before adding the next splash. Stir regularly, to release the starches in the rice that give risotto its thick creamy texture, to encourage the yellow of the saffron to disperse, and to prevent it from sticking to the bottom of the pan.

4 When the stock is all absorbed, which can be anything from 20–40 minutes depending on your pan, rice, and hob, stir in the nutritional yeast. Grate over the vegan hard 'cheese' and drizzle with extra olive oil, then leave to rest for a few minutes before serving.

Cauliflower Mac 'n' Cheese with Crispy Bacon Crumbs

Serves 4 – freezes beautifully, so grab yourself some reusable containers and get organised

————————

2 bags of smoky bacon crisps of your choosing – make sure they are vegan

½ head of cauliflower

1 red or white onion

2 tbsp cooking oil

A pinch of salt and black pepper

¼ tsp English mustard

200g macaroni or other short pasta

300ml Smoky Vegan 'Cheese' Sauce (see page 122)

This recipe is born of a cauliflower mac and cheese that I conceived for a major high-street fast-food chain a few years ago. I was standing in their head office, meeting a friend who did consultancy work there, and thinking aloud, I suggested a cauliflower mac 'n' cheese for their new menu. A few weeks later, it was one of their most successful ever launches of a new product, and at the time of writing, four years later, it is still on the menu. I should have asked for commission, but I take my cut in the glow of pride I get sitting next to someone munching one on the Underground instead.

I always meant to create a vegan version as a follow-up, and here it finally is. Instead of trying to make my own scraps of fake bacon, which is hassle and never quite hits the spot I'm looking for, I got the salty, fatty, umami smoke hit by smashing up a bag of crisps and sprinkling it on top. Careful and methodical experimentation went into this; the finalists, like an *X Factor* for maize goods, were Wheat Crunchies, Pringles, Bugles and the Co-op's version of Frazzles. All four disappear to dust when introduced to a bullet blender, mere teaspoons of salt and grease and deliciousness. Of the four, Wheat Crunchies were the surprising winner, but there wasn't much in it. Use whatever bacon-flavour crisps take your fancy, or substitute for another faux-meaty munch of your choice.

————————

Vegan(ish)

1 First smash up your crisps and set to one side. Next, finely dice your cauliflower, stalks and all, and peel and finely dice your onion. Toss into a wide, shallow pan with the oil, salt, pepper and mustard. Cook on a medium heat to start to soften the veg, but not too high that the onions will burn. Cook for 10 minutes or so.

2 Meanwhile, bring a large, separate pan of water to the boil and generously salt it. Add the pasta to the boiling salted water and reduce to a simmer. Cook for 8 minutes, then turn off the heat. It will stay warm in the water for a few minutes until the sauce is ready.

3 When the cauliflower is soft enough to gently prod a fork through, add the Smoky Vegan 'Cheese' Sauce and stir well to coat the vegetables and heat through the sauce.

4 Drain the pasta, leaving a couple of tablespoons of the salty water behind, and tip the pasta and reserved water into the pan with the cauliflower and sauce. Liberally sprinkle the crisp crumbs on top and serve immediately.

Sometimes I cook the pasta in the macaroni sauce to make things easier, but the vegan 'cheese' sauce can be volatile at high temperatures – it spits like a llama in a furious mood, so I don't recommend it here, unless you have the patience to cook your pasta very slowly and keep a measured distance from it

Beetroot and Lentil Lasagne

Serves 6–8

250g dried red lentils

1 litre vegetable or chicken-style stock – I like Osem

1 large onion

1 bulb of fennel, or 1 extra onion or 1 leek

6 fat cloves of garlic

1 tbsp cooking oil

A pinch of salt

2 large raw beetroots

2 x 400g cartons of passata or tins of chopped tomatoes

250ml red wine

2 tsp mixed dried herbs

1 box of lasagne sheets

500ml Smoky Vegan 'Cheese' Sauce (see page 122)

200g greens, finely chopped – kale, spinach or chard are best

2 tbsp breadcrumbs

rocket or green leaves, to serve (optional)

I scrub beetroot thoroughly but don't bother to peel it, partly because the skin is full of fibre and nutrients. Feel free to peel it if you want to, but make sure to wash your hands swiftly afterwards

This beetroot and lentil version is bright and beautiful, a stunning showstopper of a centrepiece on any dinner table, and packed with goodness and nutrients, too. You can use any colour lentils you like – bear in mind green and brown take far longer to cook, but hold their shape and texture better and have more of a 'meaty' bite to them. The fennel isn't mandatory – you can use a leek or onion instead if your budget won't stretch to it.

---

1 First cook your lentils; rinse them thoroughly under a cold running tap for a minute to reduce the amount of scum that accumulates when they cook. Pop them into a pan with the stock, or the same volume of water. Do not add salt. Bring to the boil, then simmer for 20 minutes until soft.

2 In a separate pan, cook the veg. Finely slice the onion and fennel, and peel and finely chop the garlic. Transfer to a large non-stick frying or sauté pan with the oil and salt. Grate the beetroots – or blitz them in a small blender or food processor – and add to the pan. Cook low and slow for 20 minutes, while the lentils simmer.

3 When the lentils are swollen and the veg are soft, drain and rinse the lentils to get rid of any scum, and tip them into the veg pan. Cover with the tomatoes and wine, add the herbs and bring to the boil. Reduce to a simmer and cook for a further 20 minutes to combine. Preheat the oven to 180°C (fan 160°C/350°F/gas 4).

4 Spread a 1cm layer of the beetroot-lentil mixture on the bottom of a 20 x 30cm ovenproof dish or roasting tin. Lay enough lasagne sheets over the top to cover. Top with a thin layer of 'cheese' sauce, then finely chopped greens. Repeat until all the mixture is gone or the dish is full, usually around four layers of pasta sheets. Finish with a layer of 'cheese' sauce, and sprinkle with breadcrumbs.

5 Bake on the centre shelf of the oven for 40 minutes, or until the pasta is soft and a knife inserted into the centre goes through easily. Serve piping hot.

Vegan(ish)

Klingon Gagh, Vegan Edition

Serves 1

———————

1 small raw beetroot, scrubbed – this is used for colour so no need to peel

1 small red chilli, plus a few slices for the top

A generous pinch of salt and grind of black pepper

100g spaghetti, linguine or tagliatelle

1 tbsp oil – I used sunflower, feel free to use something 'nicer'

1 tbsp lemon juice, bottled or fresh

When I was a child, my dad, brother and I, and my slightly less enthusiastic mum, would gather around the television set of an evening to disappear into the future aboard the *Starship Enterprise*. I grew up wanting to be, on rotation, Deanna Troi, Dr Beverly Crusher and Captain Janeway. I wore plain-coloured jerseys with black leggings and made my own *Star Trek* badges from paper and foil for fancy dress parties. Imagine my joy, twenty years later, posting a photograph of the following recipe on my Instagram account, and several fellow Trekkies delightedly pointing out its resemblance to Gagh, the Klingon, uh, 'delicacy' of live worms and seaweed. Nerdy canonisations aside, this recipe is simple to make, and so stunning to look at. It hits the spot for simple comfort in a hurry. I've left the dressing simple because sometimes you don't need any more than that. And no worms were harmed in the making of this dish, of course.

———————

1 First, half-fill a medium saucepan with water and pop it on the hob. Finely slice your beetroot, and add it to the pan, along with the chilli and a generous pinch of salt. Bring to the boil, stirring occasionally to release the beetroot juices.

2 When the water is boiling, reduce it to a simmer and slide the pasta in, allowing it to soften and easing it in gently. Or you could snap it in half and sling the lot in together, but that halves the fun of winding it around your fork and slurping it up in your face.

3 Simmer the pasta for 8–10 minutes until soft. Drain over a large bowl or jug to reserve the beetroot water – I have many uses for this, so don't throw it away (see Tip)!

4 Tip the pasta back into the pan, and dress with the oil, a little more salt, lemon juice and a generous grinding of black pepper. Serve hot with the chilli dotted on top as a treat for afterwards!

Now for that beetroot water; use it in place of water for making a simple loaf of bread with a deep russet colour and a nutty, chewy taste. Find Beet Bread on my website: cookingonabootstrap.com

Vegan(ish)

Celeriac Gnocchi

Serves 4

A decent-sized head of celeriac, around 800g

Salt and black pepper, to taste

1 tsp English mustard

4 tbsp instant mash

4 tbsp plain flour, plus extra for dusting

Oil, for greasing

Celeriac is one of the cheapest vegetables you can buy in the supermarket by the gram, but it is often unfairly maligned because of its unwieldiness and knobbly, grubby exterior. The flavour is lighter and more delicate than you would imagine on first glance, making it ideal as a vehicle for all kinds of rich sauces. This gnocchi is a hit with my friends and family, and very simple to make. If you are unaccustomed to the taste of celeriac, you can use half celeriac, half potato instead.

1 First scrub your celeriac, as much of what could be considered wastage is usually embedded soil, which will come out under a cold running tap with an old (clean) toothbrush. When it is clean, peel it, which is something of a task. Using a sturdy vegetable peeler, start from the decidedly smoother bottom half and peel it lightly, barely skimming the surface, to reduce wastage. This technique means you can go over more stubborn areas repeatedly, without taking inches of the flesh away. When it starts to get a little difficult, smooth out the knobbly bits with a small sharp knife, and carry on peeling.

2 When fully bald, slice it 2.5cm thick all over, then dice the slices. Pop the diced pieces into a pan of water, add a little salt, and bring it to the boil. Reduce to a simmer, and cook for 20 minutes, until very very soft. Drain the celeriac – retaining the hot water to cook the gnocchi in by straining it over another saucepan, and transferring it back.

3 Tip the celeriac into a mixing bowl and mash well to a smooth consistency. Stir in the mustard, and salt and pepper, and then add the instant mash and flour to form a dough. Cover it, and allow it to cool, then pop it in the fridge to chill.

Vegan(ish)

4 When cool, heavily flour your worktop, and tip the dough onto it. Divide it in two to make it more manageable, and knead briefly, incorporating more flour if it sticks to your fingers or hands.

5 Roll each dough ball into a long sausage shape and slice off rounds 1cm thick. Press with a fork to gently flatten and form the ridges that will catch the sauce.

6 Turn your oven on to 180°C (fan 160°C/350°F/gas 4) and lightly grease a roasting tin. Place it on the middle shelf.

7 Bring your pan of water back to the boil and, once bubbling, reduce to a simmer and drop the gnocchi in a few at a time. Simmer until they float to the surface, then remove with a slotted spoon and transfer to the tin in the oven to keep warm and slightly crisp at the edges.

8 Serve hot, with a sauce of your choice (see Tip).

I particularly like a simple mushroom sauce made with 400g mushrooms, 4 cloves of garlic, 1 onion and a dash of cream with this, finished with a splash of lemon juice and black pepper

Smoky Vegan 'Cheese' Sauce

Serves 4, or should.
It certainly doesn't in
my house.

———————

4 tbsp plain flour

4 tbsp light cooking oil

800ml vegan 'milk' – I prefer
cashew for this but soya
works as well

4 slices of Violife
Smoked-flavour 'cheese'

8 tbsp nutritional
yeast flakes

1 tsp English mustard

Salt and black pepper,
to taste

I use this on cooked pasta, to make a Mac 'n' Cheese baked in the oven with breadcrumbs on top (see page 115), slathered over the top of a chilli, in toasted sandwiches with Marmite, and as a dip for crisps and chips. There is usually a jar of it in my fridge at any given time, or the dregs of one. When I first nailed this recipe, I made it four days running, with no changes, feeding it to dozens of friends, all of whom raved about it. I'd go as far as to say it's the only vegan cheese sauce recipe I'll ever need again.

———————

1 First make a roux with your flour and oil by mixing them together in a medium, heavy-bottomed saucepan. I prefer to mix them off the heat and then place them on a low heat for this recipe. Add a splash of 'milk', around 3 tablespoons, then bring to a low heat, mixing well. Add a splash more 'milk' and repeat until half the 'milk' is incorporated into the pan.

2 Add the smoked 'cheese' slices and turn up the heat to medium – it is important not to boil it as plant-based 'milks' do not enjoy being boiled and they can spoil. Cook for 10–12 minutes, stirring intermittently, until the 'cheese' slices melt completely.

3 Stir in the nutritional yeast flakes and mustard, and season well with salt and pepper. Add the remaining 'milk' gradually to thin the sauce to your desired consistency and serve.

Vegan(ish)

Salad-bag Pesto

Bagged salad is one of the most wasted foods in Britain, with over half of it ending up in landfill. I have had this recipe in mind since my first cookbook, *A Girl Called Jack*, and although it is something I make for myself on a regular basis, absorbed into my household as a common staple, it has never been committed to paper until now. Bags of salad can be expensive to buy full price, but they can often be found in the reduced chiller at the supermarket, which is where I nabbed the first one I ever made this with. I like using salad leaves for pesto for variety, too, the peppery tang of rocket, the pop of colour from a beetroot leaf or baby chard, the sweet crunch of a tiny piece of spinach – and as an easy way towards five-a-day, hot and slathered all over slick, soft pasta. May the reduced stickers be ever in your favour.

Serves 6

———

150g bag of salad

1 fat clove of garlic or ½ tsp garlic paste

4 tbsp sunflower oil

4 tsp lemon juice

Salt and black pepper, to taste

To serve (optional)

300g spaghetti or linguine

2 tomatoes, finely chopped

———

1 Finely chop your salad into smithereens with a heavy, sharp knife. If you have a bullet blender or food processor you may find it easier to bung them all in here, but (on a good hands day) I enjoy the vigorous satisfaction of grinding a blade repeatedly into a bunch of leaves until they resemble a small pile of dust.

2 Pop the tiny pieces of leaf into a bowl. Peel and finely chop your garlic, if using fresh cloves, and add that too, or half a teaspoon of garlic paste.

3 Add the oil, lemon juice, salt and pepper and mix well.

4 To serve with pasta, cook the pasta according to packet instructions, then mix the pesto through the pasta and serve. You could stir through the tomatoes and extra ground pepper, if liked. Store leftover pesto in in the fridge in a clean jar, preferably sterilized (see page 23) for up to 4 days, or in the freezer for a few months.

You may want to add finely grated vegan hard 'cheese' to it to make something more closely resembling a traditional pesto, which would be a marvellous addition

Six

Big Dinners

Ultimate Moussaka

Serves 8, generously

———————

250g dried green or
brown lentils
2 small onions
6 fat cloves of garlic
2 tbsp cooking oil
1 x 400g tin of
chopped tomatoes
50ml red wine
1 tsp lemon juice or
red wine vinegar
1 tsp dried thyme or
other herbs
¼ tsp each salt and
black pepper
1 large aubergine
1 slice of bread, grated
into crumbs (to make
gluten-free, simply omit
these or use your favourite
gluten-free bread or
breadcrumb mix)
Green salad, to serve
(optional)

For the white sauce
1 tbsp flour
1 tbsp cooking oil
250ml cashew or soya milk
½ tsp English mustard

As the granddaughter of a Cypriot immigrant, I know my claim to have made the 'ultimate' moussaka is indeed a bold one. My grandfather would laugh in my face at the very notion of this vegan offering being considered anything close to the original, but, being a former chef himself (he once had a restaurant called the BellaPais, in Southend, before moving on to greasy spoon fry-ups at his guest house), his laughter would surely dissipate into an appreciative growl once he got this past his guffaws. I have long feared making moussaka, worrying it would not pass muster with my Greek bones, but tonight, I think I have cracked it. Gone are the eggs that would normally bolster the white sauce, replaced instead with unctuous cashew milk and a smattering of mustard for richness. The lamb becomes lentils, a sort of pound-shop reverse Jesus trick, and the whole thing luxuriates, dense yet sloppy, earthy yet bright, and wholesome yet decadent.

———————

1 First thoroughly rinse the lentils, then tip into a saucepan that will take double their volume, and cover them with water. Do not add salt as the skins may seize, harden and never quite cook; a rookie mistake, and an infuriating one. Bring them to the boil, then reduce to a simmer and leave to cook for 20 minutes while you make the accompanying sauce.

2 Peel and finely chop the onions and garlic, and pop into a large pan with the oil. Cook on a medium heat for a few minutes to soften, then tip in the tomatoes, wine, lemon juice or vinegar, herbs, salt and pepper. Bring it to the boil, then reduce to a simmer.

3 After 20 minutes, drain and thoroughly rinse the lentils – and I mean thoroughly – and tip them into the tomato mixture to continue to cook. Give the lentil pan a quick rinse, and use it to make your white sauce.

⟶

Vegan(ish)

4 Measure the flour and oil into the pan, and beat together over a low heat to form a paste. Add a splash of 'milk', and beat together quickly to incorporate it. Add another splash, and repeat, until you have a loose, runny mixture with no lumps. If the odd lump does occur, you can sift it out with a sieve or tea strainer, but if you don't rush it, they shouldn't be a problem. Bring the heat up to medium, and as your sauce starts to thicken, add a little more 'milk', until it is all gone. Remove from the heat and allow it to stand.

5 Check your lentil mixture – you may need to add a little water if it starts to look a bit thick. Your ideal texture is loose and sloppy but not too wet; the lentils will carry on absorbing liquid for a while yet. After the vegetable and lentil sauce has been cooking for around 40 minutes (20 pre-lentils, 20 after), remove it from the heat and stand it to one side with the white sauce. Preheat the oven to 180°C (fan 160°C/350°F/gas 4), and grab a 20 x 30cm ovenproof dish.

6 Spoon in a layer of lentil mixture to cover the base of the dish. Very finely slice your aubergine, until it is almost translucent (if you are a fan of thicker slices, you may need two, or to ration your layers!). Lay the aubergine over the lentil mixture. Spread the white sauce on top, using the back of a spoon to coat the aubergine slices. Repeat: lentils, aubergine, sauce, two or three times. Your top layer should be a layer of white sauce. Top with breadcrumbs, if using, then place in the oven for 40 minutes to bake, until golden.

7 Serve with a big green salad, if liked. Leftovers can be frozen in individual portions for easy ready meals and reheated for 45 minutes at 180°C (fan 160°C/350°F/gas 4) from frozen, or 25 minutes if defrosted.

You might ask, why not put the lentils and veg sauce in the same pot from the start? Pulses tend to give off a greyish 'scum' as they cook, which rises to the top of the pan, rather like the foam at the edges of the sea, but not quite as romantically evocative. I cook them separately to skim this off, or rinse thoroughly at the end

Vegan(ish)

Butter Bean and Cider Casserole

This soft, creamy casserole is a couple of tins of beans at their finest; simmered until gently collapsing, bolstered by rich, slow-cooked flavour. In a nod to a traditional French cassoulet, I have added a little paprika in place of the traditional bacon for a similar smoky flavour. Leftovers can be frozen, and it makes a tremendous pie filling.

---

1 Find a large, wide pan – usually known as a sauté pan, but any pan will do. Peel and finely chop your garlic, and peel and slice your onions, and toss them into the pan. Add the oil and bring to a low heat, just to knock the raw, acerbic edge from your alliums. Cook for a couple of minutes, then slice your carrots and add those too, along with the thyme. Give it all a stir and leave it on the heat.

2 Drain and rinse both tins of beans, and tip them into the pan, followed shortly by the cider, pepper and paprika. Bring the heat up to medium-high and add a third of the stock. Allow it to come to the boil, then reduce the heat to a simmer. Cook for 40 minutes, adding more stock as necessary to prevent it from drying out, as the beans will thicken the sauce.

3 After 40 minutes, finely chop the tomato, if using, and add to the pan along with the mustard and vinegar or lemon juice. Simmer for another 40 minutes, adding more stock as required.

4 Remove from the heat completely for a further 40 minutes and cover with a lid or foil, or a large plate. It will continue to gently cook in its own retained heat and save you some money in the process. Heat through just before serving and stir well – and serve up with some bread and a pile of greens.

Serves 4

---

1 whole head of garlic

2 large onions

1 tbsp cooking oil

4 large carrots, peeled

A generous pinch of dried thyme

1 x 400g tin of butter beans

1 x 400g tin of cannellini, haricot or borlotti beans – baked beans with the sauce thoroughly rinsed off work just as well

200ml cider – or white wine, if you prefer

A few pinches of black pepper

½ tsp paprika

1.2 litres vegetable stock

1 large tomato (optional)

1 tsp English mustard

1 tbsp light-coloured vinegar or lemon juice

Bread and greens, to serve

Cooking on the hob is generally the least expensive way to cook (apart from in a slow cooker, in which this recipe would work just fine with half the stock)

Spinach Dumplings in Creamy Tomato Sauce

Serves 4

200g fresh spinach, or defrosted frozen spinach

150g plain flour

1 tsp baking powder

1 tbsp grated vegan hard 'cheese'

Salt and black pepper, to taste

1 × 400g tin of chopped tomatoes

1 × 400g tin of cream of tomato soup

This simple dinner is simultaneously light but filling; when I first made it I went for seconds, and still felt brilliant … until about half an hour later, when I found myself slumped in my office chair, a human dumpling, satiated but perhaps slightly too much so! The spinach dumplings are based on Italian *gnudi* (pronounced 'nudey'!), which are usually made from ricotta, spinach and the scantest smudge of flour. These dumplings are not quite as light as those, but they are pretty good.

1 Spoon the spinach into a large mixing bowl. Add the flour and baking powder and stir through; the spinach may form into clumps, but it will all sort itself out in a moment. Add the 'cheese', salt and pepper, and mix well until the mixture starts to come together. Tinned spinach tends to be a little wet, so this will help to bind it, but if it is slightly crumbly, add a thimble of water (a teaspoon or two) and mix in.

2 Bring a pan of water to the boil, then reduce to a simmer. Form the dumplings into about twenty small balls – they will double in volume as they cook, so bear this in mind when you make them! Giant dumplings can stay raw in the middle, so there is a knack to getting them exactly the right size. I find a heaped teaspoon works just right. Ball the dough and drop it into the pan, leaving enough space for them to maraud around unhindered. Cook for 8 minutes; they will swell and float and spin in a soporific and soothing manner. Remove from the heat with a slotted spoon if you have one, or a fork if you don't, and set to one side to dry off slightly.

3 Preheat the oven to 180°C (fan 160°C/350°F/gas 4). Grab a roasting tin and pour in the tomatoes and tomato soup. Add the dumplings and bake in the oven for 20 minutes, until the dumplings are very soft and swollen.

Vegan(ish)

Slow Mole-inspired Sauce

Mole, pronounced 'mo-lay', rather than like the small reclusive animal, is a piquant and complex sauce used as the base for many Mexican recipes. I first came across it in a Mexican restaurant in Los Angeles some years ago, and longed to replicate it at home, but the process is as long as the ingredients list, and I shied away from it. This recipe is a simplification of the component parts commonly found in many mole sauce recipes, and is not, I must stress, claiming to be in any way authentic. It is simply a gateway to a new and marvellous flavour combination; but for the real experience, seek out a Mexican restaurant, or your local Wahaca, and prepare to never want to eat anything else again. I keep a jar of my cheap and relatively simple version in the fridge, to use as the base for a stew, to pep up a chilli, to smear over floury tacos with leftovers, or simply to dip chips in in front of the television.

———————

1 First peel and finely mince the onion and garlic, and pop into the slow cooker along with the chilli, cumin and cinnamon, and the oil. Cook on High for 20 minutes to start to soften the onion and toast the spices.

2 Stir in the tomato puree and cocoa powder, and cover with the stock. Replace the lid and cook on High for a further 2 hours, then remove. Pour into a blender and blend until smooth, then transfer to the slow cooker. Cook on Low for a further 8 hours, until thick, dark and glossy. It should be the consistency of cheap tomato ketchup; if it is too sloppy, simply remove the lid and turn back up to High to reduce.

3 Allow to cool completely and store in the fridge until ready to use, it will keep for a week. Reheat until piping hot.

Makes around 450ml, or a large jar. Quantities given are for a 1.3-litre slow cooker – if yours is significantly larger, please double or triple the recipe for best results, it freezes well and is very versatile!

———————

100g onion (1 large one)

2 tbsp garlic

½ tsp chilli flakes

½ tsp cumin, seeds or ground

¼ tsp ground cinnamon

1 tbsp oil

4 tbsp tomato puree

1 tbsp cocoa powder

300ml chicken-style stock, or vegetable if you prefer

Salt and black pepper

You can make this on the hob if you don't have a slow cooker. Simply cook it low and slow for an hour, allow it to cool completely, and then bring it slowly back to hot when you want to use it. It won't have quite the same depth of flavour as the slow version, but it's still delicious

Imam Baildi

Serves 2

1 large purple aubergine, the bigger the better

4 tbsp olive oil (I'm afraid it does need to be olive oil here)

A generous pinch of salt and a good grind of pepper

½ small onion, red or white

4 fat cloves of garlic

6 large ripe tomatoes

¼ tsp ground cinnamon

A pinch of grated nutmeg

Fresh parsley or mint

A handful of breadcrumbs

To serve (optional)

Crusty bread

Green salad

Imam baildi, sometimes spelled 'bayildi', is one of my all-time favourite vegetarian and vegan dishes. The name literally translates to 'the Imam fainted', although folklore argues whether this was due to the heavenly taste of the dish or the cost of the olive oil used to make it! Either way, it is succulent, flavourful, and as with all good recipes, benefits from a wealth of regional variations. Mine is based on a Greek recipe, but there are versions from Iran (with more vegetables added), Turkey, and across the Middle East and Mediterranean, each with their own flavours and twists.

1 Preheat the oven to 190°C (fan 170°C/375°F/gas 5). Halve the aubergine lengthways and place in a shallow roasting dish. Using a small sharp knife, score the flesh diagonally, taking care not to pierce the skin, the score lines should be around 1.5cm apart. Repeat in the opposite direction, to make a crosshatch pattern. Brush with a little of the oil, and a pinch of salt, and bake for 30 minutes, until the flesh is tender.

2 Remove the aubergine halves from the oven and scoop out most of the flesh. Finely chop it into very small pieces and transfer to a mixing bowl. Peel and finely chop the onion, and add to the aubergine. Grate in the garlic using the smaller holes on a box grater, or a plane grater if you have one.

3 Dice the tomatoes and add those to the bowl. Add the cinnamon, nutmeg, more salt and pepper, the herbs and another tablespoon of olive oil. Mix together well to break down the tomatoes, then spoon into the shell of each aubergine. Scatter with breadcrumbs. Drizzle with the remaining oil and a little more pepper. Turn down the oven to 160°C (fan 140°C/325°F/gas 3), and bake for a further 30 minutes.

4 Serve warm or at room temperature, with a generous salad or warm crusty bread, if liked.

Vegan(ish)

Mushroom, Lentil and Ale Pie

Serves 6 comfortably,
or 8 with sides

———————

1 large onion

6 fat cloves of garlic

2 tbsp plain flour

2 tbsp cooking oil

250ml red or dark ale

1 vegetable stock cube or
a pinch of salt

2 tbsp tomato ketchup – or
puree for the puritan palate

2 large carrots, peeled

400g mushrooms

1 x 390g tin of green or
brown lentils

1 tbsp meat-style
gravy granules

1 tsp lemon juice or
light-coloured vinegar

300g shortcrust pastry

1 tbsp cooking oil or
vegan 'milk', to glaze

Steamed greens to serve
(optional)

This pie came about because, firstly, I adore pie. It was my pregnancy craving – steak pie followed by cherry or apple pie. I would buy packets of Mr Kipling and polish them off by the half dozen. Something about the crumbling, yielding collapse of the pastry, the hot-or-cold, sweet-or-savoury, the lingering lubrication, satiation, of a layer of fat and gravy disappearing down my greedy gullet. I make a pie most weeks, more so since cooking vegan food than ever before. This particular pie came from a longing for something 'meaty', but not meat, of course. A hearty, wholesome, dark and brooding pie that would fool even the hardiest of carnivores. And so I rolled up my sleeves and got to work. This pie is something of a miracle to convert even the most hardened and sceptical carnivore – Phil, a self-confessed 'meat man' who doesn't like mushrooms, hoofed half of a very large one in one evening. When I made it for my parents, my Dad poked at it with his fork, muttering that he 'didn't eat vegan nonsense', before wolfing it down and sheepishly asking for seconds.

———————

1 First peel and slice or dice your onion, and peel and finely chop your garlic. Toss them into a large non-stick pan over a low heat. Stir in the flour and oil – it will look dreadful, but give it a chance – and bring to a low heat, mixing well to a rough, chunky paste. Add a splash of the ale, which will fizz pleasantly, and mix to loosen it. Add a splash more, mix, splash, mix, until half of the ale is combined. Set the other half to one side. Crumble in the stock cube, and ketchup or puree, and mix well.

2 Dice or slice your carrots and mushrooms, and add them to the pot. Drain and thoroughly rinse your tinned lentils, and add those too. Bring to the boil, then reduce to a vigorous simmer for around 20 minutes.

⟶

Vegan(ish)

3 When the veg is softened and the pie filling is glossy and unctuous and reduced in volume by around a third, remove it from the heat. Quickly add the gravy granules to the hot mixture and stir well, bearing in mind that they will thicken the liquid when cooked, so it can afford to be a little runny at this stage. Finish with a dash of lemon or vinegar to brighten it, as the ale can be quite a heavy, mouthfilling flavour.

4 At this point, if you are cooking the pie now, turn your oven on to 180°C (fan 160°C/350°F/gas 4) and ensure that there is a shelf in the middle of it for best results.

5 Roll out half the pastry. Lightly grease a pie tin or similar receptacle (see Tip). Lay the pastry carefully in the tin, pressing it gently into the corners. The weight of the filling will do the rest for you.

6 Spoon in the filling, working your way from the outside to the middle, and gradually so as not to overbear and thus tear your precious pastry. Fill it to the top – don't be shy – underfilled pies have their own circle in Hell in my book.

7 Now make the top. Roll out the remainder of the pastry to around 4mm thick and use cutters to create your own pie top as shown on the pictures on page 135. Carefully transfer to the dish and carefully pinch the top and base pastry together using your thumb and forefinger.

I find a loaf tin makes a very pleasing pie container in an emergency, and a Victoria sponge tin creates a thinner one with a good pastry-to-filling ratio. Leftover filling can be frozen to make future pies, or eaten as a casserole, so the size of your tin is not prescriptive

Vegan(ish)

Otherwise, you could try my idiot-proof method. I am naturally incompetent at delicate tasks, so, as with many things, I have found a method that is simple and looks astounding. I make my pie crusts with tessellated or overlaying cookie-cutter shapes. I highly recommend it – and if the pieces overlap, there is more pastry per mouthful, which can only be a glorious thing. Roll out your excess pastry to around 4mm thick. Take a cookie cutter of your choice, or if you live in a household without small children, you can use a small glass for the same effect. Cut circles of pastry and carefully lay them on top of the pie – it doesn't matter if there are gaps, in fact, they rather pleasingly get sticky with caramelized gravy, so embrace them. Start from the outside and work your way in, until the pie is covered or all the pastry is used up.

8 Glaze with a little oil or vegan 'milk'. Place it in the oven and bake for 40 minutes, or until the pastry is golden. You may wish to re-glaze halfway through, for extra sheen. I did, but then this is my living, and I need to tempt you here any way I can.

9 And serve. I found this quite sufficient on its own, my excuse for no sides being that it contained five of our 5-a-day (onion, mushroom, tomato, carrot, lentils) and because in our household, we like pie, but steamed greens work well.

Chilli Non Carne

Serves 6

2 large onions

6 fat cloves of garlic

2 tbsp cooking oil

1 tbsp smoked paprika

1 tbsp cumin, seeds
or ground

¼ tsp cayenne pepper
(optional)

½ tsp salt

½ tsp black pepper

2 x 400g tins of
chopped tomatoes

1 x 400g tin of black beans

1 x 400g tin of kidney beans

1 x 400g tin of jackfruit in
brine or water – I like
Summer Pride

175ml red wine

1 tbsp lemon juice or red/
white wine vinegar

1 tsp cocoa powder

To serve (optional)
Wedges of lime
Tortilla chips

A good chilli recipe is essential for feeding a crowd, for slinging a pile of stuff into a pot or slow cooker and forgetting about it, and for a hearty, almost effortless dinner. Serve this version with a pile of plain rice, or atop greens or salad for a healthier alternative, on buttery mash (sweet potato, polenta or plain old potato), in wraps, in toasted sandwiches, or however you please. Leftovers can be half blended, half left chunky to make a hearty, spicy soup for the next day's lunch or light dinner. This freezes wonderfully, and the flavour develops if you cook it and cool it, and warm it back through later on.

1 First peel and finely chop your onions, and peel and finely slice your garlic. Toss both into a large pan, along with the oil. Add the spices, and salt and pepper and cook on a low heat for 10 minutes to sweat the onions and soften the garlic without burning or browning them.

2 Tip in the tomatoes. Drain and thoroughly rinse the black beans and kidney beans, and add those too. Drain the jackfruit and tip it in, and pour in the wine and lemon juice or vinegar. Add the cocoa powder, and give everything a good stir. Bring to the boil very briefly, then reduce to a simmer. Cook for 40 minutes until the sauce has thickened and is glossy and dark red, and smells amazing.

3 You can serve this now, or if your timeframe and energy bill allow for it, cook it for another 20 minutes with a splash of water to stop it drying out, to really pump up the volume on the flavour front. Allowing it to cool and then blasting it back through with heat will produce a similar effect if the thought of an hour of cooking on the hob seems excessive!

4 Serve hot, but it's also delicious fridge-cold, as my midnight snacking tendencies will testify.

Vegan(ish)

Aubergine Stroganoff

Serves 2

—————

1 x 400ml tin of light
coconut milk

1 tbsp lemon juice,
fresh or bottled

1 large onion, red or white

2 tbsp cooking oil

Salt and black pepper,
to taste

1 tsp sweet paprika

4 fat cloves of garlic

1 large aubergine or
2 medium-sized ones

1 tbsp plain flour

200ml vegetable or chicken-
style stock – I like Osem

1 tsp English mustard

1 tbsp parsley leaves
(optional)

Rice, to serve

Stroganoff is a classic recipe that seems to have fallen out of fashion in recent years, but for me it is synonymous with quick and easy comfort food – creamy, gently warming and can be served atop a pile of soft pasta, mash, rice or polenta, whatever takes your fancy. Traditional stroganoff is made with sour cream, which I have emulated here with coconut milk soured with a dash of lemon juice.

—————

1 First shake the tin of coconut milk thoroughly, then open it. Add the lemon juice and stand it to one side to sour.

2 Peel and finely slice your onion, and toss into a large, wide, shallow non-stick pan. Measure in 1 tablespoon of oil, and add some salt, pepper and the paprika, and cook gently on a low heat for 10 minutes to soften.

3 Peel and finely chop the garlic and add it to the pan. Quarter the aubergine lengthways, discarding the hard greenery at the top, and slice each quarter 3cm thick all the way along. Add these to the pan, along with a second tablespoon of oil. Cook on a medium heat for 10 minutes, turning occasionally.

4 Measure in the flour and stir through briefly. Add the stock and mustard and half of the coconut milk, and bring to the boil. Reduce to a simmer for 15 minutes, until the aubergines are tender and the sauce has thickened. Add more coconut milk as required to achieve your desired consistency, and serve piping hot, topped with parsley, if liked.

Vegan(ish)

Osso Jacco

Serves 4

———————

2 large onions, red or white

2 tbsp cooking oil

1 large carrot, peeled

4 fat cloves of garlic

Salt and black pepper, to taste

2 x 400g tins of jackfruit in brine – I like Summer Pride

2 tsp plain flour

300ml chicken-style stock – I like Osem

1 x 400g carton of passata or tin of chopped tomatoes

150ml white wine

1 tsp mixed dried herbs

To serve

Chopped parsley

Grated lemon zest

I have – somewhat audaciously – based this recipe on Osso Bucco, a traditional Italian dish of veal shanks, served on the bone and cooked slowly in wine and vegetables. When I had the idea for this book, I wanted to recreate my favourite dishes from my whole lifetime so far, as simple vegan versions. Some of those proved to be extremely challenging, and Osso Bucco went on my list as a joke, at first, as I didn't imagine I would be able to recreate anything close to the original. I'm pleased to say that although not a direct replica, my Osso Jacco retains the deep ambrosial flavours that I love and the melting, rich succulence. It's a date-night dinner, a Sunday lunch crowdpleaser or a bowl of solo comfort tucked up in the corner of your favourite chair.

———————

1 First peel and finely slice your onions, then toss them into a large, shallow non-stick pan. Measure in the oil, and place on a very low heat to start to soften. Finely slice your carrot, and peel and quarter your garlic cloves lengthways, and add those too. Season with a little salt and pepper, and cook for 10 minutes to start to soften.

2 Meanwhile, drain the jackfruit and squeeze out any excess liquid by pressing it tightly between your hands over the sink. You want to lose as much of the briny water as possible, to replace it with flavour and wine, and wet jackfruit won't absorb it as well and will dilute the end result. Add the jackfruit to the pan, and stir in the flour quickly, so that it lightly coats the veg and jackfruit. Add a splash of the stock immediately, and stir briskly to prevent any lumps from forming. Add the remaining stock gradually, stirring almost constantly, to make first a thick paste and then a thinner one, and finally a liquid.

Vegan(ish)

3 Pour over the passata or tomatoes and the wine, and add the herbs. Stir everything together, then bring to the boil. Reduce to a simmer and cook for around 25 minutes, until the sauce is thick and glossy and has reduced a little.

4 To make the garnish, mix together the chopped parsley and lemon zest. Season sparsely with salt and pepper.

5 Serve hot, with a scattering of parsley and lemon on top.

Confit 'Duck' and Pear Cassoulet

Serves 4, generously

—————————

1 large onion

1 large leek

2 celery stalks

2 large carrots, peeled

1 tsp light cooking oil

Salt and black pepper

1 × 400g tin of cannellini beans – or any white beans

1 × 400g tin of haricot beans (interchangeable with any white beans)

300ml white wine, beer or cider

1 × 400g tin of chopped tomatoes, or 3 fresh

1 litre vegetable or chicken-style stock – I like Osem

1 tsp mixed dried herbs, or thyme, oregano or rosemary

1 tbsp lemon juice, fresh or bottled

200g tinned pears

A handful of breadcrumbs

For the confit 'duck'

4 tbsp light cooking oil

1 tbsp light soy sauce

1 tbsp sugar – I prefer brown

1 garlic clove, minced

¼ tsp instant coffee

¼ tsp salt

1 × 400g tin of jackfruit in brine or water – I like Summer Pride

I first cooked this recipe in a panic for *Countryfile* presenter Tom Heap and his production manager, Alistair, when they popped by my house one morning for an interview about the rise of veganism. I was billed as 'an author and chef who is making vegan food beautiful and attractive', so I put myself under an obscene amount of unnecessary pressure to create something that would live up to the hype. To add to the drama, I had spent the night before on a very slim top bunk of a juddering Caledonian sleeper train overnight from Edinburgh to London, and staggered back into my kitchen at home at 10am, with two hours to spare, an awful night's sleep, and whatever vegetables I had kicking about in the fridge to rustle up lunch with. I was quite coy about the recipe on the programme itself, not as a clever marketing ploy, but because at the time of recording I hadn't tasted it myself and I was creating it off the cuff!

I'm pleased to say this is that version, unadulterated, because we all loved it, although Tom's eyebrows almost vanished into his hairline when I told him there was instant coffee in the ingredients list! As I'm sure yours just did too … Enjoy alarming your friends with it, but make sure they take a bite first.

—————————

1 First make your confit 'duck'. Measure the oil, soy sauce, sugar, garlic, instant coffee and salt into a mixing bowl and beat well to combine. Drain and thoroughly squeeze your jackfruit between your palms to remove any excess liquid; really squeeze it out until it is as dry as possible; this will help it absorb the flavours of the marinade. Add to the marinade and mix well to cover, and pop it in the fridge until needed.

2 Separately, make your cassoulet base. Peel and finely slice your onion, and toss into a large non-stick pan. Finely slice your leek and add that too, discarding the tough green top (I keep these for making stock with, you might like to do this too). Finely slice the celery and carrots and add to the pan. Pour in the cooking oil and season with a little salt and pepper, and cook on a gentle heat on a medium sized hob ring for 10 minutes, until the veg starts to soften.

3 Drain and thoroughly rinse your beans, keeping the liquid from the cannellini beans (for aquafaba, see page 12). Add to the pan, and cover with the booze and tomatoes. Pour over 400ml of the stock, keeping the rest to one side to add as you go. Sprinkle in the herbs, and a little extra pepper, and the lemon juice or vinegar. Bring to the boil, then reduce to a simmer, and cook for 1 hour, until the veg and beans are soft and creamy. You will need to top up with stock along the way to make sure it doesn't dry out, and keep stirring intermittently so it doesn't catch and burn.

4 After the hour is up, drain the pears (I drink the juice from the tin, because I have no manners) and finely slice them. Fold them into the cassoulet and remove from the heat.

5 Spoon the marinated jackfruit into a separate frying pan with a slotted spoon, adding some of the marinade but not much of it. Fry on a high heat until crispy at the edges, then fold into the cassoulet.

6 Warm the cassoulet back through, stirring gently so as not to disturb the 'duck' too much. Serve topped with the breadcrumbs and extra black pepper.

Seven

Fakeaways

Seasoned Chick'n Poppers

Makes around 20

340g silken tofu

12 tbsp seasoning (see below)

Light oil, for cooking

Chilli sauce, to serve (optional)

For the seasoning

1 tsp salt

3 tsp mixed dried herbs

2 tsp celery salt

2 tsp black pepper

2 tsp mustard powder

6 tsp sweet paprika

4 tsp powdered garlic

2 tsp ground ginger

4 tsp white pepper

300g plain flour, plus extra for dusting

Use leftover seasoning to make 'cheese' sauce from scratch – use it instead of flour in the roux (the starter paste of fat and flour). Otherwise use it to dust burgers before frying, or to thicken stews

I made these for brunch for myself and Mrs J one weekend morning, full of a cold and too grumpy to pop to the local shop, I ransacked my kitchen cupboard to see what I could find. A carton of silken tofu and a little seasoned flour later and these tiny morsels of joy were born. We both agreed it was a mighty fine brunch, and so moreish that we weren't hungry again until dinnertime! I based the coating on a simplified blend of the eleven herbs and spices made famous by Colonel Sanders, but of course, that being a secret recipe, I can't say for sure that it's completely correct! If you find yourself missing any of the herbs or spices listed here, simply leave them out – the end result will still be delicious. The seasoning makes far more than you need for this recipe, but it does keep for a couple of months in a clean airtight jar and can be used for all manner of delights (see Tip).

1 Tip the silken tofu into a sieve over the sink to drain any excess liquid, and press it very gently – too hard and you will lose it through the sieve as it is very soft! Transfer it to a large mixing bowl and cream it with a wooden spoon or fork.

2 Mix all the seasoning ingredients together in a medium bowl. Add 6 tablespoons of seasoning to the tofu, and mix well to flavour and firm. The remaining 6 tablespoons of seasoning will become your crispy coating.

3 Take a pinch of spiced tofu, about the size of a 20p, and roll it gently in your hand. It should form a ball. If it is too tacky and sticks to your hands, add a tablespoon more flour and a little more spice. Adding more flour will temper the flavour, so for every extra tablespoon of flour you add, compensate with a teaspoon of seasoned flour. Repeat until it forms soft, doughy balls – not all silken tofu is created equal, so this is a little trial and error to get right. When you are satisfied with your tofu-dough, roll it into around 20 balls, and lay them on a lightly floured plate or worktop.

Vegan(ish)

4 Heat 1cm of oil in a non-stick frying pan until a pinch of tofu, dropped in, sizzles within seconds and floats to the top. Reduce the oil to a low heat so it does not overheat, as this can be a fire risk.

5 Taking the tofu poppers a few at a time, roll them in the seasoning and drop them gently into the pan of oil. Fry for 5 minutes, or until golden brown and floating to the surface. Remove them to a sheet of kitchen paper or a clean tea towel to absorb any excess oil. Repeat until all of the tofu is gone, and serve piping hot.

6 These will keep in the fridge for 2 days or can be frozen, uncooked, to be defrosted and cooked within a month or two.

Fakeaways

Sesame Toasts

Makes 8 pieces

————————

140g silken tofu

1 tbsp aquafaba – from a tin of cannellini beans or chickpeas (see page 12)

1 tbsp plain flour

A splash of lemon juice

1 tbsp aonori (see recipe intro on page 66)

A pinch of salt and a good grind of pepper

2 slices of white bread

1 tbsp sesame seeds

Oil, for frying

A must-have on my dinner table when I fancy a Chinese-style 'fakeaway', I tried many different iterations to make these as delicious as their prawn counterparts. I settled on this recipe; they are crisp, moreish, and a hit with my vegan and omnivorous friends alike.

————————

1 First weigh the silken tofu into a small bowl. Measure in the aquafaba, flour and a splash of lemon juice, and mix well with a fork to combine it all together. Add the aonori – this lends the fishy flavour – and salt and pepper, and mix again.

2 Spread the mixture on both slices of bread, a few millimetres thick. Scatter sesame seeds across the surface and press them in with your fingertips.

3 Slice the bread into diagonal quarters. The crusts are a matter of preference, but I like to leave them intact.

4 Heat the oil in a frying pan and when it is hot – but not smoking – add the bread, plain side down to start, and fry for a couple of minutes. Turn over and fry on the seeded side for a couple of minutes more, and serve hot.

Vegan(ish)

Crispy Seasoned Tofu

I love tofu, as a relatively new convert to the wonder of pressed bean curds, but I hear from my readers regularly that it is difficult to master, or intimidating, or that they just don't know where to start. And I empathise, because for years I felt exactly the same. I can't remember when exactly I decided to tackle it, but I'm glad I did.

1 First grab a large mixing bowl, much larger than you think you'll need, as you will want a generous amount of space to season your tofu thoroughly. Add to this the flour, paprika, herbs, salt and pepper, and mix well to make your seasoning.

2 Dice the tofu into 1cm chunks and add to the mixing bowl. Gently shake from side to side to thoroughly coat the tofu in seasoning, and set to one side.

3 Heat a large non-stick frying pan over a medium heat – not too hot – and measure in a little oil. Be careful that it does not get too hot and start to smoke. Add the tofu and cook on this heat for a minute, shaking the pan gently or, if you aren't confident about doing that, turn it gently using a fork or spoon. Reduce the heat and cook for around 10 minutes to crisp up all sides evenly, and serve immediately.

Serves 2–4, depending on what you do with it

2 tbsp plain flour

1 tbsp paprika, smoked or sweet

1 tbsp mixed dried herbs

A pinch of salt and a generous amount of black pepper

Firm pressed tofu (I like The Tofoo Co's Naked Tofoo, which is available in most supermarkets)

Oil, for cooking

You can change the seasoning ingredients depending on what is in your storecupboard; I like curry powder, all-purpose seasoning and sesame seeds. Remember to keep the flour, salt and pepper the same, as these are the bedrocks of making this both crisp and seasoned

Thai-inspired Curry

Serves 4

6 fat cloves of garlic

1 white onion

A generous thumb-sized piece of root ginger

1 tsp turmeric

1 tsp mild or medium curry powder

¼ tsp salt

A handful of coriander, plus extra leaves to garnish

1 tbsp lemongrass paste (lemon zest will do in a pinch)

1 x 400ml tin of full-fat coconut milk

2 lime leaves (optional)

400g potatoes (a waxy variety is best, but any will do, really)

2 large carrots

1 tbsp cooking oil

1 tbsp soy sauce

2 aubergines

Handful of greens

Rice, to serve

This recipe has a slightly longer ingredients list than my usual style; half of them make up the sauce, and half of them the bulk of the curry. I didn't want to cut anything out for fear of losing the components that allow me to loosely refer to it as 'Thai-inspired' in the first place – walking the line between budget cookery and honouring culinary roots is a tightrope at the best of times – so I will leave it to you to assemble it from what you have on this list. Lemon zest will do in place of lemongrass paste in a pinch, the lime leaves are delicious but can be left out, and the rest is fairly easy to find and inexpensive to pick up from local shops and supermarkets alike.

1 First peel your garlic cloves and toss them into a small bullet blender. Peel and slice the onion and add that too. Add the ginger, unpeeled, and the turmeric, curry powder and salt. Add the coriander, including the stalks, and the lemongrass paste. Blitz to a rough paste. Tip in the coconut milk and blitz again to a smooth liquid. Pour the liquid into a medium-sized saucepan with a non-stick base, and add the lime leaves, if using them. Bring to a low heat on a small ring to start to cook and thicken.

2 Scrub the potatoes and carrots, leaving the skins intact. Dice the potatoes and carrots to around 2.5cm thick, and pop them in the sauce to cook. Bring to the boil briefly, then reduce to a simmer on a medium heat, for 25 minutes, until the sauce has thickened and the potatoes are soft when pricked with a fork.

3 In a separate pan, heat a little oil and splash in the soy sauce. Dice the aubergines into 2.5cm pieces and add to the pan. Fry for a few minutes on each side on a high heat until the edges are starting to caramelize, then fold into the curry. Finish by wilting some greens with a quick stir in the pot, fish out the lime leaves, and serve.

Vegan(ish)

Fake Bake

Makes 4

---

1 large onion, red or white

2 tbsp cooking oil, plus extra for greasing

1 tbsp sugar

1 tsp paprika

½ tsp turmeric

Salt and black pepper, to taste

2 x 400g tins of jackfruit in brine or water – I like Summer Pride

3 tbsp vegan gravy granules

1 tbsp light soy sauce

320g ready-rolled puff pastry

Flour, for dusting

1 tbsp aquafaba (see page 12)

1 tbsp soy sauce

Among his many redeeming qualities, Small Boy's father, Kris, works in a famous high street bakery. I didn't quite get a fairytale ending with that one, but I did get an almost endless supply of sticky buns, and that's pretty much the same thing. So I was absolutely delighted when, in 2019, they launched a vegan sausage roll, and I launched half a dozen of them into my face in one week alone. I started to fantasize about an entirely vegan pasty-and-cake shop, and one thing led to another. I reverse-engineered this by physically dissecting a steak bake or two, then painstakingly recreating it in my kitchen at home. The jackfruit gives the tender meaty filling, the gravy fools your tastebuds into thinking it's a proper steak bake, and the rest bolsters the flavour. Bisto red gravy granules are the best to use here, and also vegan at the time of writing, but as with all things, do check the labels carefully.

---

1 First make your filling. Peel and finely slice your onion, and toss into a large non-stick sauté or frying pan. Add 1 tablespoon oil and the sugar and spices. Season with salt and pepper, and cook on a low heat for 10 minutes, until the onion starts to soften but not brown.

2 Drain the jackfruit and squeeze it in your hands to remove any excess liquid. Shred it with your fingertips until it is in fine pieces, and add to the pan. Add the gravy granules and soy sauce, and 125ml water, and cook on a low heat until the gravy has thickened. Add 125ml more water, a splash at a time, to loosen the gravy. Cook the filling for 25 more minutes, until thick and the jackfruit is tender and flavoured all the way through. Remove the filling from the heat and cool completely.

3 When the filling is cool, preheat your oven to 200°C (fan 180°C/400°F/gas 6).

⟶

Vegan(ish)

4 Divide the pastry into four equal rectangles using a large sharp knife.

5 Lightly grease a baking sheet. Place one piece of pastry on it. Spoon the filling evenly on the bottom half, leaving 1cm around the edges to prevent it from leaking out as it cooks. Carefully fold the pastry over from top to bottom, pressing the edges together gently with your fingertips. Crimp the edges with a fork, around the three non-folded sides. Repeat with the remaining three pieces of pastry.

6 In a small bowl, beat together the remaining oil, aquafaba and soy sauce to make a glaze. Brush over each pastry generously. Bake in the centre of the oven for 15 minutes, until the pastry is risen, crisp and golden.

7 Serve warm. They will keep, cooled, in the fridge for 2 days.

Vegan(ish)

Greek-style Healthier Chips

These chips are based on Greek potatoes that my Aunty Helen used to make when we were children. I've no idea if hers were low-fat or not, I was a child at the time and such questions were outside of the sphere of things I cared for, but these taste very similar. Dressing the chips in half oil, half vinegar and lemon imparts an absolute symphony of flavour, while reducing the oil content. If you care about that kind of thing. I don't, generally, but I suppose I should be mindful of it every now and then.

Serves 4

———————

500g potatoes

A generous pinch of salt and black pepper

1 tbsp flour

For the lemony dressing

100ml light cooking oil

5 tbsp vinegar – white or cider

2 tbsp lemon juice

———————

1 Leave the skin on the potatoes, and if they're a bit grubby, give them a quick clean under the cold tap. Slice thickly, around finger thickness. Cut each thick round slice into chips.

2 Pop all the chips in a large saucepan, or two if you don't have one big enough! Cover with salted water and bring to the boil, then simmer for 7–8 minutes to soften them up.

3 While the chips are parboiling, turn the oven on to 200°C (fan 180°C/400°F/gas 6), and make the lemony dressing. Pour the oil, vinegar and lemon juice into a jar with a tight-fitting lid. Add salt and pepper, and screw the lid on tight. Shake well.

4 Pour a third of the dressing into a roasting tin with deep sides, and pop it in the centre of the oven to start to warm – it's important that it's not stone-cold when the chips go in, or else they end up more soggy than crispy.

5 When the chips are parboiled, drain them thoroughly. Sprinkle over the flour and shake well to coat to absorb any lingering water. Carefully remove the roasting tin from the oven. Using a slotted spoon, carefully transfer the chips to the tray.

6 Gently toss the chips in the dressing, in the tin, and return to the oven. Cook for 20–25 minutes, shaking halfway through, adding more dressing if you want to, or saving it to use for cooking anything else. It will keep in the fridge for 2 weeks, and makes a very good salad dressing.

Crispy Chow Mein

Serves 2 generously or
4 as a side

---

4 fat cloves of garlic

2 tbsp sesame oil

2 tbsp cooking oil, plus extra
for cooking

2 tbsp soy sauce

2 tbsp rice wine or
sherry vinegar

200g meaty mushrooms —
shiitake, portobello or
oyster work, but so do
standard ones

200g dried noodles

½ head of Chinese or
Savoy cabbage

1 large carrot, peeled

1 large onion or
4 spring onions

generous handful of
beansprouts

**To make a 'meaty'
version, simply marinate
a drained can of
jackfruit in equal parts
soy sauce, rice wine
or sherry and oil for
an hour or longer. Cook
on a medium-high heat
in a non-stick pan for
20 minutes and fold
through the chow
mein to finish**

Chow mein is one of my favourite dinners to knock up in a hurry — and an excellent receptacle for odds and ends of vegetables kicking around in the fridge. Some dried noodles contain egg, so flip the packet over in the supermarket and check the ingredients. If you do struggle to find egg-free Chinese-style noodles, you can use dried spaghetti instead. It won't be strictly traditional, but it'll still be delicious.

---

1 First peel and mince your garlic, and add it to a small jar with a tight screwtop lid. Measure in the sesame oil, ordinary oil, soy sauce and rice wine, and screw the lid on. Shake vigorously to make the marinade for your mushrooms.

2 Finely slice your mushrooms and pop them in a mixing bowl, and pour over the marinade. Leave to stand for 15 minutes — mushrooms are very absorbent, so the marinade won't take long.

3 While the mushrooms soak in their dark and flavourful bath, you can cook the noodles. Bring a pan of salted water to the boil, then drop them in. Cook according to packet instructions until tender but not overdone. Drain and leave to stand.

4 Finely chop the cabbage and grate the carrot, and slice the onion or spring onions, and set to one side for a moment.

5 Tip the mushrooms into a large non-stick frying or sauté pan, or a wok if you have one, along with all the marinade. Bring to a high heat and cook for 3–4 minutes until the mushrooms start to soften. Add the drained noodles, and a splash more oil and soy sauce if needed, and turn the heat up to high.

6 Add the cabbage, onion, carrot and beansprouts, and cook for 5–6 minutes until the noodles are crisp and the veg is softened. Serve hot, but also enjoy cold from the fridge the next morning.

Vegan(ish)

✓Chinese-style Mushroom Curry

Serves 2 generously

————————

1 onion

2 tsp plain flour

2 tbsp cooking oil

2 cloves of garlic

2 tsp curry powder, as mild or as hot as you like

1 tsp turmeric

400ml vegetable or chicken-style stock – I like Osem

A pinch of sugar

1 tsp light soy sauce

400g mushrooms (see intro)

120g frozen peas

A good grind of pepper

This recipe is a firm favourite, reminiscent of the chicken curry my Dad used to dish up when I was a child; sometimes from scratch, sometimes from a jar in the supermarket, and sometimes from the local takeaway – but always, somehow, tasting exactly the same. I wanted to make a vegan version that would be just as rich, flavourful and comfortingly satisfying, and this is it. Eat atop piles of rice, or hot fat chips, as you please. Meatier mushrooms work best here, and leave them whole; keep your eyes peeled for shiitakes, oysters or baby portobellos, but in the absence of any of these, standard farmhouse mushrooms work just fine.

————————

1 Finely dice your onion and toss it into a large, wide, shallow pan, such as a frying or sauté pan. Add the flour and oil and stir well over a low heat to combine. Finely slice or mince the garlic cloves and add those too, then stir in the curry powder and turmeric. Cook all together on a low heat for a few minutes, stirring occasionally to prevent it sticking and burning. The flour and oil should form a thick paste around the onions – it's important that this doesn't burn as you'll never get the lumps out.

2 Add 100ml of the stock and stir in well, then add the rest a little at a time to thin the sauce. Add the sugar and soy sauce and stir well.

3 Gently clean any dirt from the mushrooms – I keep a small, clean toothbrush by the sink for this very purpose – and add them to the pot. Keep them whole if possible, it takes slightly longer to cook but makes for a more satisfying dinner, and looks stunning, too. Cook for 10 minutes on a medium heat until the mushrooms are cooked through, then add the frozen peas and cook for 5 minutes more.

4 Serve immediately, with a good grind of pepper to finish.

Vegan(ish)

'Egg' Fried Rice

One of the common complaints I hear about adopting a more plant-based diet is the difficulty in giving up eggs. An ideal accompaniment to the Chinese-style Mushroom Curry, opposite, this is a worthy substitute for traditional egg-fried rice — my friends and family can barely tell the difference between the two.

Serves 4 as a side dish

————————

200g long grain rice

A pinch of salt

4 tbsp gram flour

1 tsp chicken-style stock powder — I like Osem — or ½ stock cube, crumbled

1 tbsp nutritional yeast flakes

100g frozen peas

2 tbsp oil

————————

1 First soak your rice to get rid of any excess starch. Place it in a pan of cold water for half an hour, then drain and rinse thoroughly under a cold running tap, using your fingers to separate the grains well to really work it all out. Pop the rice in a large pan that will easily hold thrice its volume. Add double the volume of water to rice — I do this by weighing the rice into a measuring jug, noting the volume, and adding twice the amount of water.

2 Bring the rice to the boil, then reduce to a simmer. Cover with a lid or, if you don't have one, a dinner plate. Simmer for 18–20 minutes until soft and swollen — do not disturb it, as tempting as it may be.

3 While the rice is cooking, make the 'egg' mixture. Place the gram flour, stock and nutritional yeast into a clean jar with a tight-fitting lid. Add 160ml water and stir well to combine. Leave to stand in the fridge to thicken while the rice cooks.

4 When the rice has cooked, remove it from the heat and stir in the frozen peas. The steam from the rice will defrost them, and the frying stage will finish the job.

5 Heat the oil in a large non-stick frying or sauté pan, or better still, a wok. Tip in the rice and peas and fry on a high heat for 5–6 minutes. Add the gram flour mixture a tablespoon at a time, letting it settle for a moment before folding through so you get the nice crispy chunks interspersed throughout. Cook for a further 5 minutes, and serve immediately.

Eight

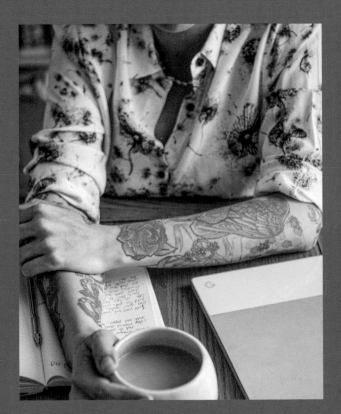

Roast Dinners

Yorkies

Makes 6, in a
deep muffin tin

———————

180g plain flour

120g gram flour

1 tsp baking powder

A pinch of salt

360ml vegan 'milk' – soya
or rice only please

180ml aquafaba – from
cannellini or haricot beans
(see page 12)

2 tsp vinegar – white wine
or cider

½ tsp English mustard

Oil, for cooking

My quest to make the perfect vegan Yorkshire puddings was years of work, and many, many failed experiments. I rarely cook the same thing more than once, as my friends and family will attest; much less likely am I to devote dozens and dozens of attempts to perfecting anything. But the vegan Yorkshire pudding was always tantalisingly within my grasp, if only for just another tweak here or there. Ordinary Yorkshire puddings are made with eggs, milk and flour. Aquafaba, the liquid from a can of chickpeas and other beans, is a common substitute for eggs in vegan cookery, but it wasn't enough on its own to hold up the humble Yorkie. I tweaked and played and tested and fiddled and finally came up with these – they are 99 per cent close to a classic Yorkshire pudding, and that's as close as I'm going to get it. *Pictured on pages 170–1.*

———————

1 Sift together the flours, baking powder and salt into a large mixing bowl. Grab a jug and pour in 180ml water, the 'milk', aquafaba, vinegar and mustard. Whisk well with a fork to combine.

2 Pour the liquid into the mixing bowl and stir to form a loose, sloppy batter. Pour back into the jug – this will make pouring it into the muffin 6-holen much easier. Pop the jug in the fridge for 30 minutes to chill and for the mixture to thicken.

3 When 20 minutes have subsided, spoon a teaspoon of oil into each cup of a 6-hole muffin tin. Heat the oven to 220°C (fan 200°C/425°F/gas 7), and place the muffin tin on the centre shelf for 10 minutes, to heat it, and the oil, to piping hot.

4 Remove the muffin tin with oven gloves or a folded-over tea towel – it will be very hot and the oil may spit, so be cautious!

5 Divide the batter equally between the 6 cups, and return the tin to the oven. Bake for 15 minutes, until risen and golden. Serve immediately.

Vegan(ish)

Jack's Legendary Roast Potatoes

Perfect roast potatoes are simply one of life's greatest pleasures — one of the soft and easy comforts that transports me straight back to a wicker chair in my elderly (and now devastatingly dearly departed) Aunty Helen's conservatory in her house in Plymouth, where I spent the summers of my childhood being chased around the garden by a large and furious goose called Charlie. Aunty Helen — as any great Greek Cypriot woman is intuitively inclined to — would feed us from the moment we awoke beneath hand-crocheted heavy blankets until the moment we crawled, satiated and delighted, back beneath the same. It was at Aunty Helen's that I learned about the birds and the bees, aged nine, leafing open-mouthed through *More!* magazine's 'Position Of The Fortnight' from a pile of women's magazines carefully concealed beneath a *Reader's Digest* in the downstairs bathroom. And it was at Aunty Helen's that the first seeds of a love of cookery were planted, standing in her galley kitchen that was filled with light, peeling so many spuds we caught the peels in a large beige washing basket; I was useless and clumsy, she was brusque but laughing with it.

I loved her so deeply, and I loved her roast potatoes most of all — especially the ones she would slice for a bedtime snack, sandwiched between two thickly sliced hunks of white bread with butter so heavy you could leave teeth marks in it, and a smudge of piccalilli to finish it off. These roast potatoes are the roast potatoes of my childhood, and a love letter to a woman I wish I could cook for now.

Serves 4

———

1kg white potatoes

A generous pinch of salt

4 tbsp cooking oil

---

1 First, lightly peel your potatoes — I swear by this cheeky little peeler with a soft grip and light touch for making a quick and easy job of it, but most potato peelers are okay. The thin metal ones are uncomfortable to grip after a while, so go for something with a bit of chunk if you want to invest in one. Anyway, lightly peel your spuds, just skimming off the skins.

$\longrightarrow$

Don't discard the potato skins – they make an excellent snack tossed in a little salt and oil and baked in the bottom of the oven

2 Cut the spuds into thirds – this is important science so pay attention. Cut the top off vertically around a third of the way in, then cut the remaining potato horizontally. This increases the amount of surface area that comes into contact with the hot oil, making for more 'crispy bit' and more consistency in the 'fluffy bit'. I have cooked literally thousands of roast potatoes and I am obsessed with this step. For overly large ones, quarter them longways for a similar result.

3 Pop your spuds in a saucepan and cover with water. Generously salt it for no real reason other than that's just what people seem to do while muttering something about bringing out the flavour. Bring to the boil and simmer vigorously for 20 minutes. Turn on your oven to 180°C (fan 160°C/350°F/gas 4) and grab a roasting tin, because the next bit needs to happen fast.

4 Pour the oil into your roasting tin. I use sunflower or vegetable, unfashionable as they may be, because olive oil is expensive and also has a low smoke point, so to more sensitive tastebuds it can have a slightly rancid aftertaste when cooked at high temperatures for a long time.

5 Drain your spuds well and tip them back into the saucepan. Shake vigorously for a few seconds to rough up the edges – this makes them extra fluffy AND extra crispy, but don't get carried away else you'll end up with instant mash.

6 Tip them into the roasting tin while still steaming and put them in the oven on the middle shelf for 90 minutes. Turn them carefully after an hour. After 1 hour has passed, scrutinize them. Do they look like the spuds in the picture? If not, return them to the bottom (the VERY bottom) of the oven for another half an hour or more.

7 After your final half hour, your potatoes should be perfect. If you find you still have other dinner things to see to, you can leave them there in the very bottom of the oven right until you're ready for them …

If you think these are in the oven
for a long time, that's the point.
In my formative years I worked in a
pub or two and quickly learned that
the reason pub roast potatoes are
so good is that they lounge in a
warm oven for half a day, gently
still cooking. (I have been known
to do mine for 3 hours, but I
mentioned that on Twitter once
and it caused a riot)

'Pork Belly'

Serves 6–8

3 × 400g tins of jackfruit
in brine or water
– I use Summer Pride

4 tbsp breadcrumbs
(1–2 slices of bread)

For the marinade
2 tbsp fennel seeds
2 tbsp coriander seeds
1 tbsp mustard seeds
1 tbsp smoked salt
1 tbsp black pepper
1 tbsp white pepper
100ml red wine vinegar
100ml black treacle or 100g
dark brown sugar
100ml cooking oil, plus
extra for greasing

For the garlic jelly
6 cloves of garlic
1 tbsp oil or vegan
spread (optional)
50ml soya milk
Pinch of salt and
black pepper
2 tbsp agar flakes

I first made this recipe as part of a dinner cooked for senior members of a TV production company who had 'bought' me at a charity auction, so I wanted to pull out all of the stops and make something truly challenging and surprising. I served a meat pork belly with the same marinade, and the vegan one alongside it. My diners were absolutely bewildered and delighted by the vegan 'pork belly', declaring it just as good as the original. I didn't get a television series out of it, but I did get a glowing sense of achievement and an excellent culinary party trick. I used sichuan peppercorns in the original, but ordinary ones will do just fine.

I am very proud of this recipe – and fully expect it to be pinched and pilfered all over the place now I've unclasped it from my bosom and released it into the wild – but will say you have to follow the method exactly to the letter the first time you make it, as a lot of work has gone into getting the flavour and texture just so. Once you've mastered it, feel free to fiddle about with the marinade, etc, but don't freestyle it then come complaining that it hasn't worked for you, because I will simply raise a tufty eyebrow, Mary Poppins style, and mutter rude things. Enjoy! I have kept exactly how to make vegan crackling to myself, however, because I have to have SOME secrets of my own.

'Pork Belly' is pictured before it goes in the oven, opposite. The finished dish is pictured on pages 170–1.

1 First make the marinade. Measure the fennel, coriander and mustard seeds, salt, black pepper and white pepper into the small cup of a small bullet blender. Add the red wine vinegar, treacle (or brown sugar) and oil. Blend for 30 seconds, pause, and blend again, so the larger seeds break down and amalgamate with the liquids.

⟶

Vegan(ish)

2 Drain the jackfruit, then squeeze it thoroughly to remove as much excess liquid as possible. Transfer the jackfruit to a mixing bowl, and shred with your fingertips so no large pieces remain. Pour over the marinade and mix well to coat. Cover and chill for 24 hours.

3 When well chilled, remove the marinated jackfruit from the fridge. Lightly grease a 20 x 30cm ovenproof dish. Spoon the jackfruit and marinade in, pressing down firmly to compact it. Place on the middle shelf of the oven at 190°C (fan 170°C/375°F/gas 5) for 30 minutes to cook.

4 While the jackfruit is cooking, make your garlic jelly. Peel and mince the garlic, and blend with 200ml water, the oil or spread, if using, and 'milk' to make a pungent, cloudy liquid. Season with salt and pepper, then transfer to a small saucepan. Bring to the boil, then reduce to a simmer, and stir in the agar flakes. Simmer for 10 minutes, then remove from the heat and stand to one side to start to set.

5 When the jackfruit has cooked for 30 minutes, remove it from the oven. Pour over half of the garlic jelly and fold through briefly – this emulates the fat that marbles through traditional pork belly, so you don't want to mix it up too much. Pour the remaining garlic jelly on top of the jackfruit, and top with breadcrumbs. Return to the oven to bake for 15 minutes more.

6 When cooked, remove from the oven and cover with foil for 10 minutes to rest – this allows the garlic jelly to cool and slightly solidify, replicating a layer of fat on top of the 'meat'.

7 Serve warm, and tender, and enjoy the reactions from your guests as you tell them that it's vegan!

Buttery Garlic Chard

I grow chard all year round – it's the only food I seem able to consistently, successfully manage to cultivate. It survives frost, snow, wind, neglect and slug invasions, and packs a hefty healthy dose of essential vitamins. It's beautiful, too – get the rainbow and rhubarb varieties for a pop of colour on your plate no matter what the season. This simple recipe is my favourite way to serve it.

———————

1 Finely chop your chard into thin strips; this is easiest if you lay the leaves on top of one another with stalks in your left hand, and roll them up tightly, then slice like a sausage.

2 Pop into a large non-stick pan. In a small bowl, mix the garlic, lemon juice, salt, pepper and oil or spread. Pour this over the chard and cook on medium heat for 5–6 minutes. Serve immediately.

Serves 2 as a side

———————

A few generous handfuls of chard

1 tbsp garlic paste (homemade or shop-bought)

1 tsp lemon juice, fresh or bottled

A pinch of salt and black pepper

2 tbsp cooking oil or melted vegan spread

Leek, Fennel, Garlic and Chickpea Mash

Serves 6

40g garlic cloves

1 large leek

½ large bulb of fennel, trimmed

1 tbsp light cooking oil, plus extra for drizzling (optional)

2 × 400g tins of chickpeas

Salt and black pepper

4 tbsp instant mash, to thicken

Splash of vegan 'milk' (optional)

I first made this for my mother-in-law as part of our Christmas dinner, dolloped inside a tremendously large bowl of light and crisp puff pastry, and topped with a lightly charred, roasted cauliflower doused in onion gravy. The whole lunch was a resounding success, but months later, she still asks me for this recipe. So Sue, here it is, just for you.

1 First peel and finely slice your garlic, and toss into a large, wide non-stick pan. Finely slice your leek, discarding the tough green tops (see Tip for uses), and add to the pan. Finely slice your fennel and add that too. Measure in the oil, and cook very gently on a low heat on the smallest hob ring for 10 minutes to soften.

2 Drain your chickpeas – reserving the liquid (for aquafaba, see page 12). Rinse thoroughly and add to the pan. Cook together for 10 minutes more until everything is soft.

3 Transfer the chickpeas and veg into a small bullet blender – you may need to do this in batches – or a food processor if you have one, and pulse until smooth.

4 Tip back into the pan, and season with a little salt and pepper. Add the instant mash to thicken, and warm through. You can add the splash of 'milk' to make it creamy if you like, and/or a drizzle of light cooking oil. Add extra black pepper to serve.

You can save the leek tops in a freezer bag to add to future vegetable stocks, if you like, to reduce food waste. I have a running bag in the top of the freezer for scraps and peels and when it's full, I boil it up and make it into stock

Vegan(ish)

A Most Excellent Nut Roast

Mrs J has been a vegetarian for two decades now, and in that period has eaten an inestimable number of nut roasts. She says repeatedly that this is her favourite 'ever', and I take that as high praise indeed. It's simple, not faffy, and the apricots can be switched out for cranberries for Christmas dinner or other seasonal occasion.

_____

1 First peel and finely slice your onions, and toss them into a large, wide non-stick pan. Add the oil, and season with salt and pepper, and cook on a very low heat on the smallest hob ring for 10 minutes, to soften without browning. When gently cooked, remove from the heat and transfer to a large mixing bowl.

2 Finely chop your nuts and chestnuts – this is easily achieved in a small bullet blender, jug blender or food processor if you have them, but if you don't, pop them into a sturdy freezer bag and grind with a rolling pin against the worksurface (the nuts, not you). Tip the crushed nuts into the mixing bowl, and add the stuffing.

3 Drain the mandarins, reserving the juice in a measuring jug, and tip them into the mix. Mash with a fork to break them up, and fold them in. Finely chop the apricots and add those too.

4 Add boiling water to the mandarin juice to make it up to 210ml in total. Pour it into the mixing bowl and stir well. Leave to stand for 15 minutes for the stuffing to swell as it absorbs the liquid. Meanwhile, preheat the oven to 180°C (fan 160°C/350°F/gas 4).

5 Lightly grease a 900g loaf tin and scrape the mixture into it, pressing down firmly into the corners to really pack it in. Leave 2.5cm from the top lip of the loaf tin as the roast may rise and expand as it cooks.

6 Place in the centre of the oven and bake for 50 minutes, until the edges are crisp. Leave to stand for 10 minutes to firm before serving. Serve warm or cold.

Serves 4, reluctantly, as I can eat the whole thing myself

_____

2 onions

1 tbsp oil, plus extra for greasing

400g mixed nuts

200g cooked chestnuts

170g dried sage and onion stuffing

1 x 300g tin of mandarins in juice

150g dried apricots

Salt and black pepper, to taste

Mandarin, Leek and Fennel Stuffing

Serves around 6,
depending on if they really,
really like stuffing

---

1 large leek

½ bulb of fennel

200g mixed chopped nuts

90g dried sage and
onion stuffing

1 x 300g tin of mandarins
in juice

This five-ingredient stuffing can be adapted to use up whatever you have in the cupboard; I have swapped the leek for onions of all colours, and the tinned mandarins for tinned pears or grated apples, depending on what I had in at the time. Use this as a bedrock recipe rather than a prescription, and feel free to adapt it to your tastes and storecupboards. It's called a stuffing, but I get away with serving it as a main course to vegetarian and vegan guests when I can't stretch to anything more complicated.

---

1 First peel and finely slice the leek, discarding the tough outer layer and the dark green tough top – I keep mine in an airtight container in the freezer to make stock or soup out of but they need a great deal of cooking to make them palatable. Finely chop the sliced leek into miniscule pieces with a large, heavy chef's knife, and transfer to a mixing bowl.

2 Grate in the fennel, wispy top included, and stir in the mixed chopped nuts. Add the dried stuffing and mandarins, including the juice, and mix well. Leave to stand for 15 minutes for the stuffing to absorb the mandarin juice and swell up – it will look a little sloppy at first, but it soon sorts itself out.

3 Turn on the oven to 180°C (fan 160°C/350°F/gas 4). Lightly grease a 20cm square tin around the edges and the bottom, taking extra care in the corners. Spoon in the stuffing. Bake in the oven for 50 minutes, or until crisp on top. Remove and cover with foil until needed, and reheat for 5–10 minutes in the oven as required.

Vegan(ish)

Beet Wellington

I have made many a vegetarian wellington, ranging from whole flat portobello mushrooms wrapped in spinach to a black bean and chestnut version, but my favourite by far is this beet wellington, and not just for its nomenclature. It requires a little care in the assembly process, but then so does a standard fillet beef wellington, and this keeps as close to the original as possible with the inclusion of a mushroom duxelles and a crepe layer. The duxelles provides a distinctive depth of flavour, and the crepe layer, although it may seem overly fancy, acts as a barrier between the vegetables and the pastry, keeping the former tender and the latter perfectly crisp. This may well be the best part of a morning's work, but the end result is more than worth it.

---

1 First make the duxelles. Peel and chop the garlic and toss into a large frying pan or sauté pan. Slice the mushrooms and onion and add those too. Measure in the herbs, and the oil, and season with salt and pepper. Cook on a very low heat for 10 minutes on the smallest burner ring on your hob, to gently sweat the onion and garlic and soften the mushrooms. Remove from the heat and transfer to a small blender or food processor, along with the chestnuts and spinach. Blitz to a smooth, thick paste. Scrape every last drop into a small bowl, and chill in the fridge until needed.

2 Next, peel the beetroots – I wear a pair of Marigolds to do this, to stop the juices from staining my fingers. Drop them into a deep saucepan, and cover with water. Add the red wine vinegar, sugar, bay leaves, if using, and salt and pepper. Bring to the boil, then reduce to a simmer for 30 minutes, until tender. Remove the beetroots carefully with a slotted spoon and pop them in the fridge to chill along with the duxelles. Boil the liquid to reduce it by two-thirds, and set it to one side.

⟶

For the duxelles

4 fat cloves of garlic

400g mixed mushrooms

1 onion

1 tsp mixed dried herbs

1 tbsp cooking oil

200g cooked chestnuts

100g spinach leaves

For the beetroot

4 large red beetroots

100ml red wine vinegar

100g white sugar

2 bay leaves (optional)

For the crepes

A fistful of spinach leaves

250ml almond, cashew or soya milk

60g plain flour

Grated nutmeg (optional)

Oil, for frying and greasing

To finish

320g ready-rolled puff pastry

1 tbsp cooking oil

1 tbsp almond, cashew or soya milk

1 tsp soy sauce

Salt and black pepper, to taste

3 tsp vegan gravy powder

3 Finally, make the crepes, which form a layer between the beets and the pastry, to keep the beets tender and the pastry crisp. Blitz the spinach and 'milk' together to make a pale green liquid. Beat in the flour, making sure to eliminate any lumps – I admit to doing this in the blender as well, while it's up and running, for speed and consistency. Season well with salt and pepper, and a little nutmeg if you have it.

4 Prepare four pieces of cling film on four side plates – a bit of a faff, but you'll see why shortly – it's good preparation for what you're about to do next.

5 Heat a little oil in a frying pan. Pour around 60ml of the crepe liquid into the pan to form a thin layer, and cover if possible with a large lid or baking tray to trap the heat. Turn the heat down low and cook the crepe gently until bubbles form on the top surface, then gently slide out of the pan onto one of the pieces of cling film. Repeat three more times to make four crepes, each on its own little prep station.

6 Remove the mushroom and chestnut duxelles from the fridge, and divide it between each of the crepes. Spread it evenly almost to the edges of each one. Place a beetroot dead in the centre of each, and carefully wrap the crepe around it, pressing it together at the top with your fingers (which will be the bottom, eventually.) Wrap each in cling film to secure it, and return it to the fridge for an hour.

7 When the beetroot-duxelles-crepe parcel has chilled, remove the pastry from the fridge and cut into quarters. Preheat the oven to 200°C (fan 180°C/400°F/gas 6), and lightly grease a baking tray. Carefully unwrap one beetroot parcel and place, messy side up, in the centre of the pastry. Fold in two opposing corners, as you would wrap an awkwardly shaped present, and then the other two. Push the pastry in gently with your fingers, and turn the

Covering crepes with a large lid or baking tray as they cook means that both sides cook without the need for flipping them over. This is a cheat I learned from an old friend on Pancake Day that I use often

Vegan(ish)

wellington over so the joined pastry is all at the bottom. Place on the baking tray, and repeat with the remaining three. Whisk together the oil, 'milk' and soy sauce in a small bowl. Brush each parcel with a little oil-milk-soy sauce mixture to glaze.

8 Bake in the centre of the preheated oven for 20 minutes, or until the pastry is puffed up, crisp and golden.

9 While the pastry heats, use the reserved beetroot and vinegar broth to make a gravy, by adding 500ml to the vegan gravy powder. At this stage of the day, you've done enough work to get away with cheating here!

10 Serve piping hot with the gravy, and veg of your choice.

Stuffed Cauliflower

Serves 4

———————

1 large head of cauliflower

1 quantity of Mandarin Fennel and Leek Stuffing (see page 178), or 2 x 85g packets of dried stuffing

Oil, for roasting

Salt and black pepper, to taste

This makes for a stunning centrepiece, especially if you use a Romanesco cauliflower in place of a plain white one. Always a hit with vegan and vegetarian friends and family, usually with other table guests asking if they can try a slice as well. Any flavour of stuffing works here, but my favourite is the Mandarin, Fennel and Leek from page 178.

———————

1 First strip away the large green leaves from the cauliflower carefully with a small paring knife, one at a time, leaving as much of the thick stalk intact as possible. Then, using a large heavy chef's knife, neatly halve the cauliflower down the centre of the thick stalk, all the way to the top. Halve these again to make four even quarters. Trim the stalk back carefully to the base of the first florets.

2 Bring a large pan of water to the boil, and salt it generously. Carefully drop the cauliflower quarters into it, and reduce to a simmer. They don't need to be submerged – you can turn them over halfway through cooking if you need to. Simmer for 15 minutes, or 20 if turning halfway through, until tender but not too soft. Remove with tongs or a slotted spoon, being careful not to break them, and allow them to steam dry and cool.

3 Make up your stuffing (see page 178, or use a decent packet of your choosing). Allow it to stand for 15 minutes to thicken while the cauli quarters cool.

4 Turn on the oven to 180°C (fan 160°C/350°F/gas 4).

5 Taking each quarter one at a time, carefully pack the stuffing around it, fingering it into the nooks and crannies between each floret, and packing it tightly between your palms. When stuffed, set into a roasting dish, and repeat with the other three. Drizzle with a little oil, and season with salt and pepper.

6 Bake in the centre of the oven for 30 minutes, until the stuffing is crisp and the cauli golden at the edges. Serve piping hot.

Vegan(ish)

Nine

Desserts

Peanut Butter Crumble Cookies

Makes 12 cookies

50ml light cooking oil, plus extra for greasing – sunflower, vegetable or rapeseed

4 tbsp peanut butter, crunchy or smooth

2 tbsp golden syrup

2 tbsp sugar

150g self-raising flour

These cookies are always very popular in my household as a quick rustle-up when I fancy a biscuit or am having a cup of tea with a friend. I sometimes replace the syrup with maple syrup if I'm feeling fancy, or black treacle if I have it in. Jam also works, for a PBJ cookie; basically, use this as a base and experiment with it.

1 First preheat your oven to 180°C (fan 160°C/350°F/gas 4), and lightly grease a large baking tray in preparation for the cookies. If you have greaseproof paper or baking parchment, you can use that instead.

2 Pour the oil into a large mixing bowl and add the peanut butter. Mix together until the peanut butter has loosened and forms a runny paste. Stir in the golden syrup, and then the sugar.

3 Add the flour, 2 tablespoons at a time, mixing well to form a smooth, glossy dough. Press it into a ball with your hands. Break off a walnut-sized piece and pop it on the baking tray. Flatten gently with a fork. Repeat until all of the dough is used up – this usually makes around 12 chunky cookies. Leave a little space between them for them to spread as they cook.

4 Bake in the oven for 12 minutes, or until golden brown. Leave to cool on the baking tray for 20 minutes to firm before attempting to move them, as they are incredibly crumbly when warm!

5 These cookies will keep in an airtight container for up to 4 days if cooled and stored correctly.

Vegan(ish)

Miso Caramel Sauce

Makes a small jar

100g white sugar

4 tbsp vegan spread –
buttery varieties work best

4 tbsp full-fat coconut cream
(see Tip, page 194)

A drop or two of vanilla
extract (optional)

2 tsp white or
brown rice miso

This caramel sauce may sound unusual, but miso is a staple flavour in both vegan and Eastern diets, adding a baseline of savoury notes known as 'umami' to a variety of dishes. Salted caramel has been in foodie fashion for around a decade now, straddling that border between completely ordinary and passé – so I've updated it here with a delicious twist. I've left the recipe just as a sauce – feel free to drizzle it over ice cream, fold it into banana cake, sandwich your favourite two biscuits together with it, pour it over pancakes, or eat it with a spoon...

1 First find a small heavy-based saucepan (see Tip).

2 Pour the sugar into the pan and place on your smallest hob ring, on the lowest heat, gently, for a few minutes, until the sugar at the edges starts to melt and turn slightly golden. Stir gently, with a wooden spoon or silicone spatula, scraping the sugar from the edges, then leave it for a few minutes more. Repeat this process until all the sugar has melted into a golden, even and glossy sauce.

3 Remove from the heat and quickly add the spread, coconut cream, vanilla and miso paste. Stir thoroughly and briskly, then return to the low heat for a few minutes. If you prefer a thinner sauce, add a little more coconut cream, but this tempers the flavour, so you may need to add more miso. Do not, under any circumstances, attempt to taste this from the pan. It's a seductive trap, and will scorch your tongue for days. I speak from experience!

4 Pour into a clean, preferably sterilized jar (see Tip on page 23), and leave to cool completely. It will keep in the fridge for 4 days, if it lasts that long!

I use a secondhand Le Creuset saucepan as its base is heavy so the caramel is less likely to stick and burn. A standard saucepan will do the job but no taking your eye off it here, else it may burn, ruining not only your ingredients, but likely your pan too. Don't be tempted to rush, making caramel is a patient affair, and the end result is worth the wait

Vegan(ish)

Bakewell Tart

This is a cross between the classic Bakewell Tart and the more familiar iced version sold in the supermarket, as I love them both equally, but including two kinds of the same cake in one recipe book could be considered a bit overexcitable. I love this cake so much that I would happily have it as a birthday cake, if only my dearly beloved weren't allergic to almonds. As it is, I make it for myself whenever she is away from home, partly so as not to kick off any throat-closures, and partly as a large saccharine comfort in her absence. You can make this as a large tart (recommended), or smaller lunchbox-sized morsels (also recommended).

---

1 Preheat your oven to 200°C (fan 180°C/400°F/gas 6).

2 Next, make your pastry. Grab a large mixing bowl, and sift together the flour and icing sugar. Add the vegan spread a tablespoon at a time, so it goes in in dollops, which will be easier to work with. Rub the flour, sugar and spread together between your fingers to form a fine, breadcrumb-like texture. When all the spread is incorporated, add the cold water 1 tablespoon at a time, mixing thoroughly with the handle of a fork or a rounded butter knife acting as a dough hook, to combine.

3 Lightly dust your worktop with a blend of flour and icing sugar – I sift mine for an even coating. Pop the dough onto it, and knead briefly for a minute or two, then roll it to 5mm thick.

4 Lightly grease a 20cm tart tin (or use a shallow 20cm cake tin if you don't have one). Carefully lift the pastry up and place it in the tin, allowing the edges to overhang, which will allow for shrinkage. You can trim them later.

5 Loosely cover the pastry with foil, and fill with baking beans. If you don't have baking beans, large dried beans or chickpeas will do the same job. Bake on the centre shelf of the oven for 12–15 minutes.

⟶

Serves 6–8

150g vegan spread – buttery varieties work best

150g caster sugar

½ tsp almond essence

100ml 'milk' – it makes sense to use almond, but any will do

1 tsp white vinegar or lemon juice

100g plain flour

2 tsp baking powder

150g ground almonds

4 tbsp strawberry or raspberry jam

2 heaped tsp icing sugar, plus extra for dusting

2 tbsp flaked almonds (optional)

For the pastry

190g plain flour, plus extra for dusting

15g icing sugar

100g vegan spread, plus extra for greasing

3 tbsp ice-cold water

6 Remove the tart base from the oven and carefully remove the foil and the beans. Return it to the oven for 12 minutes to cook further.

7 Once cooked, remove from the oven and leave to cool, in the tin. Once cool enough to handle, trim any overhanging pastry edges with a sharp knife, and discard. (I blitz them in a small bullet blender and pop them in a jar to use as sprinkles for ice cream, mixed with sugar and cinnamon, because I cannot bear waste. It's good, you should try it!)

8 To make the filling, add the spread and sugar to a small saucepan, along with the almond extract. Place on the smallest hob ring on the lowest heat to melt the spread for a minute, stirring to prevent it catching and burning. Remove from the heat as soon as the spread is melted, add the 'milk' and vinegar or lemon juice, and set to one side.

9 In a large mixing bowl, sift together the flour and baking powder. Stir in the ground almonds. Make a well in the centre and pour in the liquid, mixing well to form a smooth batter.

10 Spread the jam over the pastry base, using a pastry brush or the back of a teaspoon to get it into the edges, but carefully, as you don't want to damage your pastry. Pour the batter over the jam, and sprinkle the flaked almonds on top, if using.

11 Pop the tart back in the oven for 18 minutes, or until a small sharp knife inserted into the centre comes out completely clean. Leave to cool for 30 minutes before removing from the tin and placing on a wire cooling rack, with greaseproof paper or a tray underneath it.

12 Make up your glaze by mixing the icing sugar with 1 teaspoon of water. Mix together and add more water until it reaches the desired consistency. Drizzle the glaze across the top of the tart, generously – the excess will fall through the cooling rack and onto the paper or tray. Repeat as desired, and finish with more almonds, if you like.

Vegan(ish)

Millefeuilles

Serves 4

2 x 400g tins of coconut milk, chilled in the fridge overnight to firm up and separate

200g icing sugar, plus extra for dusting

1 tsp xanthan gum

150g fresh strawberries, or thereabouts

1 x 300g ready-rolled puff pastry sheet

Cocoa powder, for dusting (optional)

Until I was writing this book I had no idea what these were called. I would just point at it in the bakery window and ask for 'the layer cake thing'. In researching how to make these, and then working out my own vegan versions, I had to learn how to not only make them, but also how to spell them, and how to pronounce them. It's 'mee-fwoy', or as near as damn it. I tend to use Jus-Rol or supermarket equivalents on busy days, because life is short, and most ready-made pastries are both vegan and foolproof. These are utterly delightful.

1   Carefully remove the lids of the chilled coconut milk and scoop out the hardened cream (you should be left with 200g from both tins). Reserve the coconut water (see Tip).

2   Heat the oven to 180°C (fan 160°C/350°F/gas 4).

3   Pop the hardened coconut cream into a mixing bowl, and add the icing sugar and xanthan gum. Whisk well to form a thick cream, and place in the fridge until required. Finely slice your strawberries and set to one side.

4   Unroll the pastry sheet on its greaseproof paper and prick all over with a fork. Lightly score the sheet into twelve even rectangles. Bake in the centre of the oven for 15 minutes, until risen and golden. Remove from the oven and allow to cool completely, before slicing into fingers with a large, heavy chef's knife.

5   Place one finger of pastry on a plate. Spoon on a little of the coconut cream. Top with strawberries, then pastry, then cream, then strawberries, then a final layer of pastry. Dust with icing sugar and a little cocoa powder to serve, if liked.

Tip

Pour the reserved coconut water into a jar to use in a future recipe, such as soup, or adding to a bread dough in place of water, or to make a curry – there are plenty of options

Vegan(ish)

Coconut, Lime and Strawberry Puffs

Makes 12

———————

1 x 400g tin of coconut milk, chilled in the fridge overnight to firm up and separate

12 frozen puff pastry vol-au-vent cases

6 tbsp lime marmalade

1 tbsp xanthan gum

100g icing sugar, plus extra for dusting

Fresh strawberries, to serve

These originated as an idea for cheat-millefeuilles but grew a life of their own as I dolloped them with lime marmalade and snacked on them as I wrote up recipes one spring afternoon. I ended up keeping them as an entirely separate simple recipe in their own right, and developed the millefeuille in a more traditional manner (see page 192–3) The xanthan gum can be found in the baking aisles of large supermarkets, and as well as a thickener for stubborn coconut milks, it can be used in gluten-free baking to help bind bread and make it less crumbly. It's an unusual ingredient by my ordinary standards, but a fairly useful one.

———————

1 Carefully remove the lid of the chilled coconut milk and scoop out the hardened cream (you should be left with 100g). Transfer the solid milk into a mixing bowl. Reserve the coconut water (see Tip on page 192).

3 Now, heat your oven to 190°C (fan 170°C/375°F/gas 5). Lightly grease a baking tray and place the vol-au-vent cases on it, evenly spaced apart. Place them in the oven to cook according to packet instructions.

4 Add a tablespoon of the reserved coconut water to the solid milk and whip until well combined. Add the lime marmalade, xanthan gum and icing sugar and beat to form a thick creamy liquid that can make soft peaks. If it is too thick, add another tablespoon of coconut water to thin it, but you want it fairly thick.

5 When the pastry cases have cooked, remove them from the oven and place in the freezer for 10 minutes to cool. Top with the coconut lime cream.

6 Finely slice each strawberry and perch on top of the cream. Dust with a little icing sugar, and serve.

Vegan(ish)

Mint Choc Chip Ice Cream

This simple method has revolutionized my ice-cream making; especially vegan ice cream. In fact, I see no reason to ever go back to the chore of whipping and gently folding egg whites into creamed yolks and sugar, beating in cream, hoping it doesn't collapse… I've dispensed with the whole hullabaloo of it all, and made it super simple. You can whip it for an even lighter, fluffier version, but this feels decadent, unctuous and creamy. By its nature, this ice cream contains far less fat and sugar than traditional ice cream does. In fact, it's basically perfect. Enjoy!

1 Strip the mint leaves from the stalks and pop them in a small bullet blender. Add the coconut cream, peppermint and golden syrup, and pulse to a pale green colour. Add half of the chocolate chips and pulse again.

2 Pour the mixture into an ice-cube tray (I prefer a silicone one for ease of popping them back out again), making sure you scrape every last drop from the sides of the blender and the blades. Pop it in the freezer for 4 hours to set.

3 When hard, remove and pop out each cube into the blender again. Pulse briefly to combine, or if you don't fancy washing the blender again you can mix it in a mixing bowl with a fork, but you'll have to be quick so it doesn't start to melt!

4 Fold in the remaining chocolate chips then scrape it into a Tupperware. Return the mixture to the freezer for 15 minutes to reset, and serve. Enjoy quickly, with the knowledge that you are never more than a moment away from good, reasonably healthy, vegan ice cream.

Serves 2

A generous fistful of mint

250g coconut cream
(see Tip)

1 tsp peppermint extract

2 tbsp golden syrup

100g dark chocolate chips

There are three main kinds of coconut products in the supermarket and it's important to get the right one for this recipe. You want coconut cream, not coconut milk and not creamed coconut. Coconut milk is too sloppy and won't set properly; creamed coconut is rock solid and won't do very much at all. Coconut cream is a halfway house between the two, an entire carton of the thick clotted coconut at the top of the tin of a can of coconut milk

Biscoff Ice Cream

Serves 2–4

150g Biscoff biscuits

400g creamed coconut, or the thick top of a can of coconut milk (2 x 400ml tins is sufficient)

3 tbsp golden syrup

Of all of the hundreds, if not thousands, of dishes I have made for Small Boy and Mrs J, both of them instantly declared this to be 'the best' of all of them. And that's quite some compliment indeed. Mrs J despises coconut, detects it in absolutely anything I try to smuggle it into, but the Biscoff was a sufficient disguise for it here, so if you aren't a huge coconut fan, bear that in mind and perhaps give it a go. I have piled this into a KnickerBiscoff Glory, sandwiched it between Biscoff biscuits for the ultimate warm-weather snack on the fly, and eaten it straight from the blender. My friend Georgi suggests pouring a shot of espresso over it like an affogato, and she's usually right. I hope you love it as much as we do.

1 First grind the biscuits to dust in a food processor or bullet blender. If using a bullet, you will need to do them in batches and for no more than 30 seconds at a time else the motor may overheat. I lost a blender in the making of this recipe, and yet, I have no regrets. If you don't have a blender, you can use the traditional method of popping the biscuits in a freezer bag and attacking them with a rolling pin, but this yields a slightly more grainy ice cream. Still delicious, but not quite as wonderful as the ice cream that I want you to have.

2 When the biscuits are dust, add the creamed coconut and golden syrup and combine well. Spoon the mixture into an ice-cube tray or two, depending on the size of them. Freeze for 2 hours.

3 Once frozen, turn out and combine with a wooden spoon or by tipping back into the blender for two 30-second pulses. Transfer to a Tupperware container. Return it to the freezer for 15 minutes to firm up. Serve and enjoy.

4 This ice cream sets very hard in the freezer, so if you aren't going to eat it immediately, remove it for 10 minutes before serving and mix it well to soften it up.

Vegan(ish)

Lime Marmalade Ice Cream

Serves 2–4

———————

400g coconut cream
(see Tip, page 194)
200g lime marmalade

My first memory of lime marmalade was standing in my nan's galley kitchen as a child, firkling around in her fridge for a sneaky snack in the way that children do, and always will do. I pulled the jar from the fridge door – Rose's Lime Marmalade – and stared at it. It was squat, and the contents a clear, pale, yellowy green colour. I unscrewed the lid and eyed it with a mixture of suspicion and delight. I don't think I had ever tried a lime before. I stuck a finger in (sorry, Nanny Joan!) and my eyes almost popped out of my head with delight at the sweet, tangy, unfamiliar flavour, with the tiny shreds of lime peel like sour chewy sweets, sticking to my teeth. As I started to write this recipe as an idea for my book, it was as though a portal in the universe had opened and I had fallen headfirst back into my nan's kitchen, aged six or seven, with my fingers in the jam jar. I knew I had to make this, and the marmalade has to be Rose's. If you can't find it, Tiptree Lime is also excellent.

———————

1 First spoon the coconut cream into a small bullet blender. Add the lime marmalade and blend until well combined.

2 Pour the coconut-lime mixture into an ice-cube tray and pop it in the freezer for 4 hours to set. Eat any leftovers clinging to the edges of your blender cup, because it would be rude to waste a drop of this, and unlike traditional ice-cream recipes, there are no raw eggs or other nonsense in there to do you a mischief.

3 When the ice cream is set, pop out the cubes and back into the blender. Pulse briefly to combine them, then scrape it into a Tupperware and return to the freezer for 15 minutes.

4 If you aren't going to serve this immediately from the second set, and I appreciate that it is quite an organisational feat to decide to make ice cream exactly 4 hours and 15 minutes before you fancy it, simply remove it from the freezer for 10 minutes before serving to allow it to soften up.

I have made this with tiny dark chocolate chips studded throughout as well, which is nice, but I prefer the palate-cleansing simplicity of the original

Vegan(ish)

Tiramifu

When I announced to my readers that I was writing a vegan recipe book, I was overwhelmed with requests for a tiramisu. You know, that classic, rich, Italian dessert made with eggs, cream, and all sorts of non-vegan ingredients. I made it my mission to make one that would rival my favourite, eaten in my early twenties at *Il Pescatore* restaurant in Southend and never forgotten. I had been stood up on a date, and, dolled up and crushingly alone, I decided to order dinner anyway, with a confidence that evaded me for the following decade and only seems to be returning now. I hoped I was giving off an air of casual sophistication, but my mascara-stained, hot cheeks hinted otherwise. I ordered a limoncello sorbet for dessert, and one of the staff, whose name may have been Eric, brought me a portion of tiramisu as well, as almost an unspoken consolation.

Eric's act of kindness made the tiramisu one of the greatest desserts I had ever eaten, and I have loved it ever since. This recipe is not a tiramisu, because to call it such would be to do an injustice to all those I have loved before, but it is a tirami*fu*.

---

1 First bake your cake, assuming you don't have any lying about. For best results for the tiramifu, place the mixture from the Vegan Birthday Cake recipe (see page 216) in a lightly greased and lined 900g loaf tin. Heat the oven to 180°C (fan 160°C/350°F/gas 4) and bake the loaf cake on the middle shelf of the oven for around 25 minutes or until risen, pale but gently golden and a small sharp knife inserted into the centre comes out clean.

2 Remove the cake from the oven and make twenty small, evenly spaced holes throughout the cake using a skewer, pressing all the way to the bottom.

⟶

Serves 4 generously

---

1 quantity of Vegan Birthday Cake mixture (see page 216)

2 tbsp good-quality instant coffee

4 tbsp strong coffee liqueur (optional)

1 tsp sugar

340g silken tofu

200g coconut cream (see Tip, page 194)

1 tsp vanilla extract

175g icing sugar

½ tsp xanthan gum

Cocoa powder, for dusting

2 Spoon the instant coffee into a small mug and add 200ml boiling water. Stir well to combine. I would ideally use cold espresso from my stovetop Bialetti, but in the real world it's more likely to be strong instant coffee. Sweeten with the 1 teaspoon sugar and stir well. Pour the coffee over the cake in the tin and let it soak in. Leave to cool completely on a wire cooling rack, then gently lift from the tin.

3 While the cake is cooling and soaking, make the cream layer. Tip the tofu and the coconut cream into a small bullet blender, along with the vanilla. Blend to a smooth, creamy, thick liquid. Add the icing sugar and xanthan gum and blend again to combine. Pour into a mixing bowl and whisk to form soft peaks, then chill in the fridge until required.

4 Cut the cake into slices around 2.5cm thick. Place one on a plate, and cover thickly with the cream. Place a second slice on top, and repeat. Dust with cocoa powder to finish.

Vegan(ish)

Beanjuice Meringues

I first tried these meringues using the sludge from a can of chickpeas, known in vegan circles as aquafaba, and used as an egg replacement in all kinds of recipes – from glazing pies, to scones, to meringues. I just couldn't shake the background taste of chickpeas, and I didn't like them at all, unfortunately. So I set about trying to make them with a different aquafaba; and cannellini trumped them all by miles. I make these with a combination of caster and icing sugar; caster for the science, and icing sugar for a glossy fondant smoothness. Sometimes I replace half the caster sugar with brown sugar for a caramelly-sticky centre, but only when I feel like showing off.

Makes 10 small nests

___

1 x 400g tin cannellini beans – or 125ml aquafaba (see page 12)

Oil, for greasing (optional)

180g caster sugar

20g icing sugar

½ tsp xanthan gum

1 tsp arrowroot powder

1 tsp lemon juice

___

1 First drain the beans, catching all of the liquid in a jug or bowl beneath. Set the beans to one side to use in another recipe – see the index at the back of the book for ideas.

2 Preheat the oven to 110°C (fan 90°C/225°F/gas ¼). Line a couple of baking trays or cookie sheets with greaseproof paper, or lightly grease them, and set them aside.

3 Measure the aquafaba – you need 125ml – any excess can be stored in a jar in the fridge, to be used as a pastry glaze or as a thickener for sauces as required.

4 If you have a bullet blender, mix the sugars together to a fine powder to combine them; it helps to create a smoother finish. This isn't an essential step but it does make for a cleaner, glossier meringue, if you care about that kind of thing.

$\longrightarrow$

5 In a large mixing bowl, whisk the aquafaba with the xanthan gum using an electric whisk until white and fluffy. This is quite hard work when whisking an egg by hand, so if you don't have an electric whisk be prepared for a workout! Add the sugar, 2 tablespoons at a time, and continue to beat well. When most of the sugar is added, drop in the arrowroot powder, then the lemon juice a little at a time, still beating, to stabilize the mixture. White wine vinegar works too, but rather like chickpea water, the taste somewhat lingers, and savoury meringues aren't particularly popular for a reason! (Although typing that sentence has sent me on a belligerent imaginative tangent, so watch this space, I guess.)

6 Beat the mixture until, rather like ordinary meringue mixture, it forms stiff peaks. Dollop onto the baking trays and bake for 1 hour and 20 minutes. Leave in the switched-off oven to cool for a further hour, then remove and serve.

Ten

Puddings

Bread-no-butter Pudding

Serves 4–6

4–6 slices white bread

30g vegan baking spread, plus extra for greasing

4 tbsp mixed dried fruit

4 tsp sugar, plus extra (optional)

1 tbsp flour

1 tbsp light cooking oil

300ml vanilla soya milk

½ tsp ground cinnamon

Not strictly a bread and 'butter' pudding, as the butter in this case is a vegan baking spread, but I kept the name for nostalgic purposes. You can make your own vanilla-soya milk by mixing 1 teaspoon of vanilla extract into 300ml soya milk, or you can buy it ready made. I have taken liberties with the custard element, but regular readers will know by now that I take liberties all over the place, and should be unsurprised. It's unorthodox, but it works, and that's all that matters.

1 First preheat your oven to 180°C (fan 160°C/350°F/gas 4).

2 'Butter' your bread with the baking spread, and cut into triangular quarters. Lightly grease a deep 20cm square tin, and lay pieces of bread on the bottom, covering as much of the tin as you can. Sprinkle 1 tablespoon of mixed fruit on top, and 1 teaspoon of sugar. Repeat to make four layers, or until all the bread has been used up.

3 Heat the flour and oil together in a small saucepan and whisk to make a roux. Add a splash of the vanilla 'milk' to loosen. Add a splash more, whisking all the time, and a splash more, until the 'milk' is all incorporated. This makes an approximation of custard, which works just as well as ordinary custard for this purpose. Add the cinnamon and remove from the heat.

4 Pour the 'custard' over the bread. Sprinkle with a little extra sugar, if you like, to brown the top. Place in the centre of the oven and bake for 30 minutes or until golden and the custard is all absorbed. Serve hot, or cold, as you like.

Vegan(ish)

Red Rice Pudding

I am a huge advocate of using cheap ingredients and have been
making rice pudding with supermarket value-range long grain
rice for years, much to the chagrin of some of my more pedantic
readership. Yet every now and again something comes along that
is the exception the the rule – we are all complex human beings,
after all – and this is one of them. I hold fast on not caring for
arborio rice in risotto, but the nutty, rich flavour of red rice makes
this pudding utter comfort-food heaven. You can, of course, make
it with regular long grain rice, or pudding rice, if you can't find or
don't see the point in the red rice, but my rule of thumb is if I'm
not wasting money on animal products, which are frequently the
most expensive items in the weekly shop, I can afford to splash
out on a fancy grain every now and again.

Serves 2

120g red rice

2 x 400ml tins of coconut
milk, chilled in the fridge
overnight to firm up and
separate

100g sugar

A few drops of vanilla
extract

Jam or frozen berries,
to serve

---

1 Carefully remove the lids of the chilled coconut milk and scoop
out the hardened cream. Pour the watery coconut milk into a jug
and set aside.

2 Pour the rice and the watery coconut milk into a medium-sized
saucepan – heavy-bottomed or non-stick are the best as it will be
cooking for a while. Bring to the boil, then cover and reduce to a
simmer for 40 minutes, stirring it every now and then to stop it
sticking and burning.

2 When the rice has absorbed almost all of the coconut milk,
add the hardened cream, sugar and vanilla and stir through well.
Pour into an ovenproof dish and bake at 140°C (fan 120°C/275°F/
gas 1) for 45 minutes, stirring halfway through.

3 Serve with a dollop of jam on top, or if you're feeling fancy, stir
through some frozen berries a few minutes before the end and
allow them to stew gently.

Sticky Gingerbread Fingers

Makes 12 generous fingers

———————

225g soft vegan spread, plus extra for greasing

225g soft brown sugar

225g black treacle

4 tbsp apple sauce

300ml 'milk' – almond or cashew work best here

350g plain flour

2 tsp grated fresh or ground ginger

2 tsp ground cinnamon

2 tsp bicarbonate of soda

These simple spiced fingers are delicious warm or cold, and make an excellent portable snack. This recipe is based on a traditional one from *Leiths Cookery Bible*, but with a few tweaks to make it vegan. I found that cashew and almond milk work best, but those with nut allergies can use rice or oat varieties instead.

———————

1 First lightly grease a 20 x 30cm deep cake tin, or one of similar proportions. Line it with greaseproof paper if you have any to prevent the cake from sticking to the sides and enable it to be removed cleanly, but if you don't have any, just grease the tin well, taking extra care to lubricate the corners.

2 Preheat your oven to 150°C (fan 130°C/300°F/gas 2).

3 Weigh the spread into a large mixing bowl. Add the sugar and cream together to make a kind of buttercream. Pour in the treacle gradually and beat well to incorporate it, then repeat with the apple sauce. It looks a little ghastly at this stage, but bear with it. Pour in the 'milk' little by little, beating constantly to loosen. If you have a bullet blender, I admit to putting the spread, apple sauce, 'milk' and treacle in together and blasting to a liquid, then stirring in the sugar, but if you don't, it's no bother, just do it the old-fashioned way.

4 Add the flour, ginger, cinnamon and bicarb, and mix well to form a smooth batter, with the ingredients evenly distributed throughout.

5 Pour the batter into your prepared cake tin. Bake for 50 minutes to an hour, or until the cake is risen, a dark golden colour, and a sharp knife inserted into the centre comes out clean.

6 Remove from the oven and leave in the tin for 20 minutes to firm and cool, before slicing into fingers, to serve. Will keep for 3 days in an airtight container, or 3 months in the freezer.

Vegan(ish)

Two-ingredient Berry Bread Pudding

I made this as an emergency pudding for a dinner party for twelve strangers, having travelled forty miles with a rucksack of vegan pulled pork marinating in Tupperware containers held together with duct tape and carrier bags to stop any spillages as I navigated three trains and hundreds of bored, furious commuters en route. I arrived and unpacked my bag and realised that the pudding I had made was still sitting on the side in my own kitchen, forty miles and three trains away. Thinking on my feet, I rummaged in the freezer department of the local corner shop and found a bag of dubious frozen berries and asked my host if he had, and I quote, 'any cheap white bread kicking around'. Lo and behold, he produced a loaf of squashy, supermarket air and nonsense, and I set to work. I made enough for two puddings; one for the assembled guests, and one for my host and his family to enjoy the next day. It was a resounding success, and one I will no doubt pull out of the bag many, many times in the future.

Serves 6–8

400g frozen mixed berries
8 slices of cheap white bread
Vegan spread, for greasing

---

1 Pop the berries in a medium-sized saucepan and bring to a medium heat – do not boil them as you will spoil the flavour. Cook the berries – with or without sugar, see Tip – for around 15 minutes, until they are well softened and juicy. Remove from the heat and spoon out 2–3 tablespoons to serve on top of the pudding. Set aside.

2 Cut the bread into quarters, and then each quarter into quarters again, so each slice is in sixteen pieces. Drop them into the saucepan – no point in dirtying a mixing bowl for this job – and mix well to absorb all of the juices from the berries. The bread should swell and all turn a lurid purpley pink colour. Leave the bread soaking for 15 minutes, stirring it occasionally to break it up and allow it to absorb evenly.

⟶

I deliberately didn't add any sugar to my recipe, preferring a more tart pudding, but you may wish to taste your berry mixture and make your own decision, as some of the bags of frozen berries have a greater quantity of cranberries or blackberries, which can change the flavour somewhat

3 Preheat your oven to 180°C (fan 160°C/350°F/gas 4). Lightly grease a cake tin – a 20cm one will do, round or square – and spoon in the mixture. Press it down with your fingers to compact it tightly into the tin, and carefully tip off any excess juices that come to the surface – this is a very moist pudding, but it needs to be able to cook and set!

4 Pop it into the oven for 40 minutes, until slightly risen and caramelized on top, and firmish to touch. Remove from the oven and allow to cool in the tin for 10–15 minutes before serving topped with the reserved juices.

I served this with a rosewater custard – a carton of fresh custard mixed with some rose petals I had at home (Oatly do a great vegan 'custard'). But corner shop tinned custard and a splash of rosewater does the job just nicely

Vegan(ish)

Orange and Almond Brownies

Makes 9 generous brownies

————————

5 tbsp sunflower oil, plus
extra for greasing
200g dark chocolate
170g ground almonds
2 tbsp cocoa powder
200g caster sugar
A pinch of salt
1 orange
230ml almond milk
1 tsp orange extract
200g whole blanched
almonds

I am utterly obsessed with these brownies; they're so dense and sweet and sticky and moreish, and also vegan and gluten-free. I add orange flavouring to mine, but they also work with caramel, peppermint or lemon extract.

————————

1 First preheat your oven to 180°C (fan 160°C/350°F/gas 4). Lightly grease a 20cm square baking tin with a little oil, then line with greaseproof paper, leaving a little overhang at the edges.

2 Measure 5cm of water into the bottom of a medium-sized saucepan and place a heatproof bowl over the top. Lift it off again and check that the bottom is still dry, as you don't want the water to touch the bowl and scorch the chocolate. If it is, you're good to go. If not, tip a little out and try again. Place the pan of water, with the bowl in place, on a medium heat and bring to the boil. Reduce to a simmer. Break the chocolate into the bowl and melt it gently, adding the oil, and stirring intermittently.

3 In the meantime, measure the ground almonds, cocoa, sugar and salt into a large mixing bowl. Mix well to evenly distribute the ingredients. Zest your orange using the small rounded holes of a box grater, a plane grater or zester, and set to one side.

4 Pour the almond milk, and the melted chocolate, oil and orange extract into the dry ingredients and stir well to make your brownie batter. Fold in most of the almonds and orange zest, setting some of each to one side to scatter on top.

5 Pour the mixture into the prepared tin, spreading it out into the corners and smoothing the top. Scatter over the remaining almonds and orange zest. Place into the oven for 22–25 minutes, or until cooked on the outside and cracking at the top, but not jiggly when you shake the tin gently from side to side.

6 Leave to cool for 15 minutes before gently removing from the tin by pulling out the greaseproof paper at each side of the tin and lifting the whole lot onto a cooling rack. Slice and serve.

Vegan(ish)

Birthday Cake

Serves 6–8

300g plain flour
2 tsp baking powder
½ tsp salt
300g sugar
1 x 400ml tin of full-fat coconut milk
90ml cooking oil
1 tbsp lemon juice
2 tsp vanilla extract

For the icing
375g icing sugar
225g vegan spread – I use Pure
2 tbsp vegan 'milk'
Sugar sprinkles, to decorate

This simple cake recipe can be customised however you like – I have made it with peanut butter icing and strawberry jam slathered between the layers, and as a chocolate cake by adding cocoa powder and blackcurrant jam, but my favourite iteration is as a classic vanilla sponge with 'butter' icing and jam, and multicoloured sprinkles all over – a kitsch and understated classic in a world of ever more ridiculous showstopper cakes, and a hit with adults and children alike for all occasions.

1 First heat your oven to 180°C (fan 160°C/350°F/gas 4) and, if your shelves move, place one slightly below the centre. Lightly grease two 15cm round sandwich tins.

2 Sift together the flour and baking powder into a large mixing bowl, and add the salt and sugar. Stir well to combine.

3 Shake the can of coconut milk well to combine it. Measure it into a jug and add the oil, lemon juice and vanilla. Pour into the mixing bowl and whisk well to make a smooth, lump-free batter.

4 Divide the mixture evenly between the two cake tins. Bake in the centre of the oven for 22–25 minutes, or until risen, pale but gently golden and a small sharp knife inserted into the centre comes out clean.

5 Remove from the oven and place, still in the tins, on a wire cooling rack to settle for 20 minutes. Remove carefully from the tins and place on the wire rack to cool completely before icing.

6 To make the icing, mix the icing sugar and vegan spread, and thin with your chosen 'milk'. Sandwich the cake together with some of the icing when cooled, and spread the remainder evenly over the top and around the sides, using a palette knife to smooth around the edges and the top. Liberally cover in your chosen sprinkles, and enjoy.

To speed up the sponge-cooling process and prevent your buttercream from melting, leave the cake to cool for 40 minutes then place carefully in the fridge for 2 hours or the freezer for 30 minutes. This cools the surface, making the application of icing far simpler and less disappointing

Vegan(ish)

About Jack Monroe

Jack Monroe is an award-winning food writer and bestselling author. Books include *A Girl Called Jack*, *A Year In 120 Recipes*, *Cooking On A Bootstrap* and *Tin Can Cook*. She has won the Fortnum & Mason Food and Drink Award; the *Observer Food Monthly* Best Food Blog and Food Personality of the Year; *Marie Claire* 'Woman At The Top'; *Red Magazine*'s 'Red Hot Women'; the YMCA Courage & Inspiration Award; the Woman of the Year Entrepreneur Award; the Women of the Future Media Award and many more. She works with and supports The Trussell Trust, Child Poverty Action Group, Plan Zheroes, The Food Chain and countless food banks, schools and children's centres, teaching people to cook and eat well on a low income and campaigning against the causes of poverty and austerity in Britain and abroad. She lives in Southend-on-Sea, Essex, with her partner and son, and a large ginger cat.

Acknowledgements

Thank you to Carole Tonkinson, my patient and trusting publisher, and the whole Bluebird team at Pan Macmillan who helped bring this book to life. Martha Burley for gentle email reminders to get on with it, and Hockley Raven Spare, Zainab Dawood, Jess Duffy, Jodie Mullish and Sarah Badhan. Thanks to Pip Spence and Patsy Niven for the food styling and photography. To Caroline for all of her assistance in helping eat the recipes as I created them, and also for keeping me as organised as it's possible to (which is: not very!) To Rosemary Scoular for still being by my side on this wondrous and often exasperating journey, and Aoife Rice and Natalia Lucas at United Agents. And finally, to Louisa and Jonathon, for all your love, support, clean plates and understanding (mostly) when I need to lock myself in the office and write like a dervish. Here's to all the future books, and may you all forever be on this rollercoaster with me – my team of wonder women – keeping my arms and legs inside the cart, and all that.

Index

Vegan(ish)

Vegan(ish)

First published 2019 by Bluebird
an imprint of Pan Macmillan
The Smithson, 6 Briset Street, London EC1M 5NR

Associated companies throughout the world
www.panmacmillan.com

ISBN 978-1-5290-0508-0

9 8 7 6 5 4 3 2 1

A CIP catalogue record for this book is available
from the British Library.
Printed and bound in China.

Publisher Carole Tonkinson
Managing Editor Martha Burley
Editorial Assistant Zainab Dawood
Senior Production Controller Sarah Badhan
Design Andrew Barron / Thextension
Hand Lettering Mel Four
Prop Styling Cynthia Blackett
Food Styling Pip Spence and Lizzie Harris

Visit www.panmacmillan.com to read more about all our books and to buy
them. You will also find features, author interviews and news of any author
events, and you can sign up for e-newsletters so that you're always first to
hear about our new releases.